CONTENTS

Introduction to this book

INTRODUCTION TO THIS BOOK

In the main, those who have bothered to pick up this book will be people who want to know more about marriage and divorce or civil partnerships and dissolution or have experienced an initial separation from their partner and are now considering taking the first steps towards finalizing divorce/dissolution. The book will also concern those who wish to know more about the Civil Partnerships Act 2004 and civil unions. It has been a few years since the advent of the Civil Partnerships Act so the question of dissolution of partnerships is now relevant as quite a few couples have decided to dissolve their partnerships.

Marriage or civil partnerships can be wonderful institutions and are fine until things go wrong. Everything associated with separation and divorce or dissolution is usually traumatic and hurtful to those involved. This book does not attempt to deal with the more personal aspects of divorce and dissolution, such as the sense of failure and sense of loss. However, what it does do is offer a more practical insight into how the divorce/dissolution process works on a legal level and how you can prepare yourself adequately for these final steps towards ending your marriage/partnership.

As you begin the process of getting divorced, or dissolution, you may feel that, rather than go rushing immediately to a solicitor, you want to gain a clearer picture of what lies ahead and a background knowledge of the procedures involved. You might even want to do a lot of the work yourself, in order to keep costs down and to exercise more control. Getting divorced, or experiencing a dissolution of a civil partnership will usually involve a lot more than simply obtaining a decree, which announces that your marriage/partnership is over. There will, in most cases, be questions surrounding children, property, money etc. From this book you will gain a practical insight into the law surrounding the divorce process and also how these other matters are resolved. A word of caution: it should be remembered that in certain situations it will not be advisable to do it alone without the use of a solicitor. Such cases will be where children and assets are involved and negotiation is needed, or where there are other conflicts.

This book deals with the institution of marriage to begin with and in Chapter 11 covers civil partnerships in detail.

1

Marriage and Cohabitation

The law of England states that marriage is the 'voluntary union for life of one man and one woman to the exclusion of all others'.

Much has changed in family life over the years and today, marriages break up with alarming frequency and more and more people choose to live together as opposed to marrying.

This section is about the institution of marriage and how it works within the law. We will look at who can get married, the engagement, marriage formalities, effects of marriage, cohabitation and agreements.

Marriage

The law states that, in order to marry, a person must:

a) be unmarried
b) be over the age of 18

You are also legally a single person if your previous marriage has been annulled. Basically, anyone who wants to marry must be a single person in the eyes of the law. A person must be over 18. If a person is aged between 16-18 parental consent must be gained. A marriage where one of the persons is under 18 is absolutely void, unless parental consent has been gained. If someone marries between the ages of 16-18 the marriage is voidable as opposed to void (see below). Parents, guardians or the courts must consent to a marriage for someone between 16-18 years old.

The Civil Partnerships Act 2004 has introduced civil unions between same sex partners. Through a Civil Partnership, people of the same sex will acquire many of the rights of a conventional married couple. See chapter 11 on civil partnerships. However, the law of conventional marriage specifies that the marriage must be between partners of opposite sexes.

No marriage can take place between close relations, i.e. blood relations, or non-blood relations where the relation is so close that a ban on intermarriage is still imposed. Adopted children are generally treated in law as blood relatives. Brothers in law and sisters in law can marry as can stepparent and stepchild if the stepchild has not been raised as a child of the family and is over 21 years old.

Marriages must be voluntary

A marriage must be voluntary and not brought about through coercion. This brings about a problem in law when arranged marriages take place, as is the custom in certain ethnic groups. In general the law does not interfere with arranged marriages.

However, the courts will get involved if it is felt that there is duress and there is a threat of injury to life or liberty or a child is threatened with expulsion from home or community.

Marriages which can be annulled

Void marriages

Certain marriages are regarded in law as void. This means that, in the eyes of the law the marriage has never taken place at all. Marriages are void where:

- one of the parties is under 18
- the parties are closely related

- one of the parties is not a single person, i.e. the marriage is bigamous or polygamous.
- The parties are regarded in law as being of the same sex.

Certain marriages are regarded in law as valid until they are annulled. These are 'voidable' marriages and, in the eyes of the law can be annulled by either party.

Grounds for annulment

In order for a court to annul a voidable marriage the following grounds have to be demonstrated:

a) the marriage has not been consummated
b) the husband or wife had not understood the nature of the ceremony
c) the marriage was to someone of unsound mind
d) the marriage was to someone with venereal disease.

Getting engaged to be married

An engagement is not a precondition of marriage, as it once was. This is often the case, however. A couple will, after engagement, publicly announce their intention to be married. Legal disputes can, however, arise and couples can dispute ownership of property and gifts. An engagement ring is regarded as an outright gift in the eyes of the law.

If money has been expended on larger items, such as a house, in the anticipation of marriage, and the marriage has fallen through then this will become a legal dispute with each case turning on its own merit and the circumstances of any contract, written or unwritten. Certain insurance companies can offer insurance against weddings falling through or being cancelled. Cover can also be obtained for honeymoons falling through.

If a couples wedding falls through they are legally obliged to return any wedding gifts received to their senders.

Marriage formalities
For a marriage to be valid, a formal licence and a formal ceremony are necessary. Authority to licence marriages is given to a priest of the Anglican Church and to civil officials (registrars). Every couple, therefore, must obtain permission to marry from an Anglican church or from a civil official. Many couples, because of cost, choose to marry in a registry office.

Religious ceremonies
Religious ceremonies are categorized according to whether they are solemnized by:

- The Anglican Church, including the Church of Wales
- Jews or Quakers (for whom special rules apply under the Marriage Act 1949
- Some other recognized religion.

We have lived in a diverse ethnic society for many years and the rules governing marriage and religion are largely outmoded and in need of change. This will inevitably happen over time.

Church of England-licence to marry
About half of all religious marriage ceremonies take place in the Church of England. There are four ways to effect the necessary preliminaries for an Anglican marriage. Only one may be used. In order to obtain consent to marry in the Church of England you must either:

- publish banns

or obtain one of the following:

- a common ecclesiastical licence
- a 'special licence, also from the ecclesiastical authorities
- a superintendent registrars certificate from the civil authorities.

Publishing banns

The banns, or the names of the couple who intend to marry, have to be read aloud (published) in the church of the parish where the couple are resident. If the couple are resident in different parishes then the banns must be read in each parish church, in one or other of which the ceremony will take place. The priest needs seven days notice in writing from both parties before the banns can be read. The priest has to read them audibly in church on three successive Sundays. If there is no objection from any member of the congregation then, after the third reading the marriage can take place. If any objections are raised, and voiced audibly by a member of the congregation then the banns are void.

Common licence

This dispenses with the banns and is given by the Bishop of the diocese. You must make a sworn affidavit that there is no impediment to the marriage and that any necessary parental consent has been given and that you have resided in the parish for 15 days.

Once granted, the licence to marry has immediate effect and is valid for three months. It will specify the church or chapel in which the marriage is to take place.

Special licence

This is issued by the Archbishop of Canterbury and enables a marriage to take place at any time or place. It also dispenses with the 15-day residence period. To get such a licence, which would for example be applicable if one of the parties was seriously ill, a sworn statement is required.

Superintendent registrars certificate

Although it is the norm for a marriage in the Church of England to take place after banns have been read, or after obtaining a licence from church authorities, an Anglican wedding can take place after a superintendent registrars certificate has been obtained. The parties must give notice to a superintendent registrar in the district in which they have resided for at least seven days before giving notice. They must make a solemn declaration that there are no lawful impediments to their union and that they meet the residential requirements. In the case of persons between 16-18, that they have parental consent. If the parties live in different districts then notice must be given in each district.

The notice is displayed in the superintendent's office for 21 days. At the end of that period, provided there are no objections, the certificate is issued. The marriage can take place in a church within the superintendent's district. The consent of the minister of the church must be obtained.

Divorced person wishing to marry in the Church of England

Where either party is a divorced person, a remarriage cannot be solemnized in the Church of England. This does not apply where the marriage has been annulled.

Other stipulations to a Church of England wedding are laid down in the law, as follows:

- the marriage must be in an unlocked church
- between the hours of 8am and 8pm
- two witnesses must be present

Other denominations and religions

If you belong to another denomination or religion other than the Church of England, you must first obtain permission from the civil authorities to marry. There are four ways of meeting the legal requirements, of which only one need be used:

- a superintendent registrars certificate
- a superintendent registrars certificate with a licence. This has a residence requirement of 15 days.

For those seriously ill or detained, special provisions under the Marriage Act 1983 and the Marriage (Registrar General's Licence) Act 1970 will apply.

Weddings for Jews and Quakers can take place anywhere or at any time under the Marriage Act according to their own practices. The marriage is solemnized by a person designated for the purpose.

Civil ceremonies

The General Register Office will issue a form 357, which provides notes on the legal formalities of marrying. Marriages in a register office require a solemn declaration from both bride and groom according to the civil form:

- that they know of no impediment to their union
- that they can call upon those present as witnesses that they take each other as lawful wedded wife or husband.

The two witnesses present then sign the register.

The superintendent registrar and the registrar must both be present at a civil wedding, which can only take place in a registry office, except in very unusual circumstances where people are ill or otherwise confined.

Witnesses

All marriages, without exception, be they religious or civil, require two witnesses to the ceremony. The witnesses need not know the couple. After a ceremony the witnesses sign the register and a marriage certificate is issued.

Marriages abroad

Generally speaking, a marriage that takes place in another country is recognised as valid in this country. However, all the laws associated with marriage in England and Wales, must apply, such as the age restriction and the single person status. It is essential if a person intends to marry abroad that they seek legal advice in order to ascertain the status of the marriage in the UK.

Effects of a marriage

Being married confers a legal status on husband and wife. In general, questions of status, rights and duties concern the following:

Duty to live together

Husband and wife have a duty to live together. If one spouse leaves the other for good then an irretrievable breakdown has occurred (see next chapter on divorce).

Duty to maintain

Spouses have a duty to maintain one another. This extends to children, obviously, and becomes a particular problem on breakdown of marriage.

Sexual relationship
Husband and wife are expected to have sexual relations. Failure to consummate a marriage, as we have seen, can lead to annulment of a marriage.

Fidelity
Husband and wife are expected to be faithful to one another. Adultery is one of the main grounds for divorce.

Surnames

A wife can take her husbands surname but is not under a legal duty to do so. A wife's right to use the husbands surname will survive death and divorce. A husband can also take a wife's surname although this is unusual. Occasionally, couples will adopt both surnames. If a wife changes her surname to her husbands she can do so informally, simply by using the name. However, change of surname has to be declared to institutions such as banks and a marriage certificate has to be produced.

Joint assets

The matrimonial home as well as family income become assets of a marriage. As we will see, a breakdown of marriage can lead to long and costly battles over assets of a marriage.

Common parenthood

Husband and wife automatically acquire parental responsibility for the children of their marriage. If the couple separate the courts can alter the relationship between parent and child.

Marital confidences

Secrets and other confidences of married life shared between husband and wife are protected by law. This is particularly relevant in this day and age where the tabloids invade the lives of people as never before. Married, and even divorced, persons can obtain injunctions to stop publication of confidential information.

Marriages of convenience

The laws surrounding such marriages have been gradually tightening up. Such marriages are seen as sham devices to get around UK immigration law. In order to issue a person with an entry clearance certificate to enter the UK as an affianced person or spouse, the immigration authorities will want to be sure that:

a) the 'primary' purpose is to get married and that a separation will not take place after marriage and entry
b) that spouses intend to live together as husband and wife
c) if the couple are not already married that the marriage will take place within six months.

It also has to be shown that parties to the marriage will settle in the UK.

Cohabitation

Despite peoples perceptions to the contrary, there is no such thing as 'common law' relationships, i.e. people living together unmarried, as man and wife. As far as the law is concerned they are two legal individuals. There is no duty to cohabit, no duty to maintain. With regard to children, the duty of care usually falls on the mother. However, in the case of unmarried couples, both mother and father can enter into a parental responsibility agreement which should place them in a similar position to married couples in regards to responsibility for children.

If a couple who cohabit and have children, do separate then there is a duty on the father (absent parent) to maintain the child until they reach the age of 17.

Effect on assets

The courts can decide what split will take place in regard to assets of a cohabiting couple. This share is based on concrete facts of the individual's contributions. A live-in partner has no right to occupy the family home under the Matrimonial Homes Act 1973, in the event of breakdown of relationship. However, the law has tightened up in this area. See the chapter on divorce.

Taxation

There are important differences between the tax position of married and cohabiting couples. These are as follows:

- cohabiting couples cannot take advantage of the taxation rules between husband and wife that ensure gifts between husband and wife are free of capital gains tax
- they cannot take advantage of the fact that on the death of a spouse, the other spouse inherits free of inheritance tax

However, as these rules change frequently you should refer to your local tax office for advice. You should also take advice concerning wills and pensions.

Where the law treats cohabitees as husband and wife

There are certain areas where the law will afford the same protection to cohabitees as married people:

- Victims of domestic violence are entitled to protection whether married or not
- With regard to security of tenure, a couple who live together as husband and wife will be entitled to joint security whether married or not
- Certain social security benefits are available for live in couples. You should seek advice from the local benefits agency
- A duty to maintain the children of a relationship is imposed-irrespective of whether married or not
- Under the Fatal Accidents Act 1976 dependant cohabitees, who have lived together for two years or more may be entitled to damages on his or her death.

Agreements

Cohabitees can enter into agreements to protect property and other assets in the event of splitting up. Married couples also do this.

Contracts between married couples

At common law, a husband 'administered' his wife's property. In effect, a woman no longer owned property after she married. The law moves on thankfully! Today, property that a woman owned before marriage remains her own. If divorce takes place the question to be considered is whether the property has become an asset of the marriage. Each case will turn on its own merit.

In view of the courts wide powers to determine what happens to assets after marriage, few couples enter into agreements (pre-nuptial agreement being the most common). However, the wealthier the person, the wiser it is to enter into such an agreement.

Prenuptial agreements

Prenuptial agreements were not traditionally regarded as binding by the English divorce courts, but there are signs of change. One factor behind this is the increasingly international character of people's lives. So saying this, the main aim behind prenuptial agreements is that, for at least one of the parties to marriage, be it man or woman, may wish to preserve previously acquired assets from the jurisdiction of the divorce courts. Unfortunately, the situation in almost all cases is that the jurisdiction of the courts cannot be ousted in this way and prenuptial agreements are quite often not worth the paper they are written on.

The agreement will be considered in the light of exactly how long the marriage has lasted and also whether or not there are children involved. English courts traditionally would say that the husband or wife should part with some of the pre-existing wealth if the assets built up over a marriage did not suffice to provide for children's well being.

One relatively recent case which serves to highlight the changes referred to is that of Radmacher v Grantino. Mr Grantino, a French national, married Ms Radmacher, a German national in 1998. The marriage lasted until 2006. They had two children by their marriage. Ms Radmacher belonged to a wealthy industrial family. They came to live in England and sought a divorce in England. By the time of the divorce it was estimated that Ms Radmacher was worth 100m. Much of the wife's wealth had been given to her by her family during her marriage. Prior to the marriage, the wife's family were concerned that none of the wealth should go to her husband so an agreement was drawn up, in a German court. This was drawn up in German, and in the context of German law and Mr Grantino had no real input into the agreement. At the time of the divorce Mr Grantino was claiming 5m for himself and children to ensure that the children were cared for. The court of appeal stated that adults ought to be free to make their own arrangements. They decided that although Ms Radmacher should buy her husband a house he would only have the right to occupy it while the children were dependant.

The case then moved onto the Supreme Court who upheld the view of the Appeal Court and that Mr Grantino should be held to the terms of the prenuptial agreement. However, this case involved millions of pounds whereas most don't and the courts will continue to look at prenuptial agreements on their own merits.

Cohabitation agreement
When unmarried couples part, the courts have little powers to determine the split of assets. In relation to cohabitation agreements, there are problems under the law of contract. When parties enter into a contract, both sides have to offer something towards the contract. This is called 'consideration' for the contract. In an agreement to cohabit it would be difficult to define consideration other than on the basis of a sexual relationship. Nevertheless it is wise to have an agreement as a basis, or structure, of the relationship when it concerns assets.

2

Divorce-Main Principles of the Law

Divorce law generally

Divorce law has developed over the years through legislation made by Parliament and through the build up of "precedents" or through cases decided by the courts. However, in the last thirty years there have been fundamental changes in the way society, and the law, has come to view divorce.

Modern divorce law recognizes that "irretrievable breakdown" of a marriage should be the one and only ground for divorce. This recognition signalled a move away from the idea of "guilty parties" in divorce.

Before the introduction of the notion of irretrievable breakdown it was held that one party had to prove that the other party was guilty of destroying the marriage before divorce could be granted. The law is now much more flexible in its recognition of the breakdown of a marriage.

Since the present law was introduced, making it much easier to obtain divorce, the number of marriage breakdowns in Britain has risen significantly, with one in three couples filing for divorce. This is currently the highest rate in Europe.

There are a lot of problems associated with the law, and the role of those who make divorce law generally. The whole question of divorce law is under scrutiny, particularly the question of whether or not the law should attempt to keep marriages intact or whether it should seek to ease the transition to final separation without presenting unnecessary obstacles. However, although we hear periodic announcements from different politicians on the importance of keeping the family unit intact, and by implication making it harder for people to divorce, the whole climate has changed over the years whereby the law seems to be the facilitator of divorce as opposed to dictating whether or not people can get a divorce.

There has also been a major shift in the law concerning children of divorcing couples. Under The Children Act 1989 (as amended), parents in divorce proceedings are encouraged to take the initiative and take matters into their own hands, making their own decisions concerning the child's future life after divorce. The courts role has been greatly restricted. (See chapter 4)

The Child Support Act 1991 (as amended by the 1995 CSA) has also dramatically changed the role of the courts in divorce proceedings. The Child Support Agency, assesses and determines applications for maintenance in accordance with a set formula (see chapter 5) The courts will only now deal with applications for maintenance in certain circumstances.

Law generally – the courts
Before looking at the law surrounding divorce in greater depth, we should look briefly at the structure of the courts and how divorce law is administered.

County courts
Most divorces are handled by a branch of the county court system known as the divorce county courts.

County courts are local courts, usually found within towns and cities throughout England and Wales. These courts do not deal with criminal matters but they attempt to find solutions to virtually every other type of problem facing people in every day life. Such problems might be those that arise between businesses and their customers, between neighbours and between landlord and tenant, to name but a few.

Not all county courts are able to deal with divorce, those that can are known as divorce county courts. Decisions concerning divorce cases, and subsequent orders, are made by Judges and District Judges. These people are appointed from the ranks of senior lawyers. In addition to the judges there is also a large staff of officials who provide the administrative machinery of the courts. Like all administrators, they are the backbone of the operation.

In London, the equivalent of the divorce county court is known as the "Divorce Registry" and is based in the Royal Courts of Justice in the Strand.

The High Court

Sometimes, rarely, divorce cases need to be referred to the High Court. There are several sections of the high court-the section responsible for divorce and other similar matters is known as the Family Division. However, the majority of divorce cases will be heard in the county courts.

Hearing your divorce case

Hearings related to divorce cases are either in "Open" court or in "Chambers". Proceedings in open court are heard in the court-room itself. They are usually formal and members of the public are allowed to attend. However, most divorces are heard in chambers. These proceedings are private and the general public has no right to attend or listen. Only those people directly concerned with the case are allowed to attend.

Seeking your divorce – the grounds for divorce.

The first question facing couples that wish to divorce is whether or not they qualify at the outset to bring proceedings, i.e., what are the ground rules. If one or other parties wishes to file for divorce, the most basic requirement that must be fulfilled is that they should have been married for one-year minimum. They must also be "domiciled" in this country. Both parties must have their permanent homes in England or Wales when the petition is started or both parties should be living in either England or Wales when the petition is started. If this is not the case then both parties must have had their last home in England or Wales when the petition is started or must have been living in England or Wales for at least a year on the day the petition is started. There are a few other stipulations concerning domicile. Leaflet D183 which can be found on the www.justice.gov.uk website explains domicile in depth.

A court can halt proceedings for divorce in England if it would be better for the case to be heard in another country. Usually, the court would try to decide which country is the most appropriate, or with which country the divorcing couple are most closely associated.

Grounds for divorce – the 'five facts'.

As we have seen, there is only one ground for granting a divorce, that is the irretrievable breakdown of marriage. Fundamentally, this means that your marriage has broken down to such a degree that it cannot be retrieved and the only solution is to end it legally. (Matrimonial Causes Act 1973).

The person, or spouse, who requests a divorce is known as the "petitioner". the other party is known as the "respondent".

Although there is only one ground for divorce, the court has to be satisfied that there is clear evidence of one of the following five facts:

1. that the respondent has committed adultery and the petitioner cannot, or finds it intolerable, to live with the respondent;
2. that the respondent has behaved in such a way that you cannot reasonably be expected to live with him or her (unreasonable behaviour)
3. that the respondent has deserted you for a continuous period of two years immediately before the presentation of your petition for divorce.
4. that parties to a marriage have lived apart for more than two years prior to filing for divorce and that there is no objection or defence to filing for divorce. This is known as the "no fault" ground;
5. that parties to marriage have lived apart continuously five years prior to filing for divorce.

Since the advent of the 1996 Family Law Act, it has been proposed that the above five facts are replaced with a single ground for divorce. However, although the Act came into force in July 1997, the changes to the divorce procedures have yet to be effected. Therefore, from hereon, we will refer to the practice as it currently stands. We should now look at each of these "five facts" in more depth.

1. Adultery
Quite simply, adultery is defined as heterosexual sex between one party to a marriage and someone else.

Adultery usually means that a "full" sexual act has been committed so therefore if there has not been penetration then this will not be seen to be adulterous.

For adultery to be proved, an admission by the respondent or evidence of adultery is usually sufficient. The co-respondent need not be named in the divorce petition. If you do mention the name of the co-respondent involved in the adultery, that person is entitled to take part in the divorce proceedings in so far as they affect them. The court will provide the co-respondent with copies of all the relevant divorce papers and he or she will have the opportunity to confirm or deny anything said about him or her in the divorce proceedings. Proving adultery is the first step. You then have to satisfy the courts that you find it intolerable to live with the respondent any further. However, it is not essential to prove that you find it intolerable to live with the respondent because of their adultery. It may be that your marriage has been unhappy for some time and that the adulterous act has proven to be the end. If, after you discover the respondent's adultery, you continue to live together as man and wife for a period of six months or more, you will not be able to rely on adultery as a reason for divorce. As long as the periods of living together after the adultery do not exceed six months in total, the courts will completely disregard them. This gives some room for attempts at reconciliation.

2. Unreasonable behaviour

Although "unreasonable behaviour" is a commonly cited fact for divorce, in practice the court has stringent criteria, which must be met before this is accepted. The law actually says that you must demonstrate that your spouse has behaved in such a way that you cannot reasonably be expected to continue to live with that person.

The court considering your case will look at the particular circumstances surrounding your situation and will then decide whether or not you should continue to tolerate your partner's behaviour within marriage.

The main principle underlying unreasonable behaviour is that it is particular to your own situation and that it cannot be seen as relative to other people's behaviour.

You must prove that the behaviour of your partner has gone well beyond the kind of day-to-day irritations that many people suffer and there is real reason to grant a divorce.

Examples of such behaviour range from continuous violence and threatening or intimidating behaviour, drunkenness, sexual perversions, neglect, and imposing unreasonable restrictions on another person.

3. Desertion

The fact that you must prove that your spouse has deserted you for a continuous period of two years can present difficulties.

If you are seeking a divorce on the basis of desertion, then it is likely that you will need to employ a solicitor who will need to check rigorously that you comply with the (often complex) requirements upon which a court will insist before granting a divorce. In the main, desertion has arisen because of other associated problems within marriage, and therefore this factor can often be joined with others when applying for a divorce

The simplest form of desertion is when one person walks out on another for no apparent reason. Desertion, however, is not just a physical separation of husband and wife. It implies that the deserting party has rejected all the normal obligations associated with marriage.

Before desertion is proven a court will need to be satisfied of two things:

1. You must demonstrate that you and your spouse have been living separately for a continuous period of two years immediately before you started the divorce proceedings. Although it is usual for separation to start when one person leaves the marital home, it can also happen whilst you are living under the same roof, but living totally separate lives.

The courts are very rigorous indeed when determining that this is the case and will need to be satisfied that your lives are indeed separate and

27

that you can no longer go on carrying out functions jointly. The court will disregard short periods during the separation where you may have attempted to patch up your differences. However, for example, if you attempt to reconcile six months into the initial two year period and this lasts for two months before you separate again, although the courts will not make you start again they will make you wait a further two months before they will hear your divorce. Therefore, the two years becomes two years and two months.

2. That your spouse has decided that your marriage is over-you must also be able to demonstrate that when he or she stopped living with you, your spouse viewed the marriage as ended and intended to separate from you on a permanent basis.

You will not be able to claim desertion if you consented to the separation. The court will take consent to mean that you made it clear from the outset that you consented to separation, through your words or actions.

In addition, you will not be able to claim desertion if your spouse had perfectly good reason to leave, for example he or she may have gone abroad with your full knowledge, to work or may have entered hospital for a long period.

If your spouse leaves because of your own unreasonable behaviour, then you cannot claim desertion. If you are to blame in this case, the courts will not accept desertion.

Finally, because the courts see desertion as essentially separation against your will, then if you come back together again on a permanent basis you can no longer claim desertion.

4. Separation for two years with consent

As with desertion, the particular circumstances in which the law looks upon you as having been separated for two years can include periods of time where you may have been under the same roof together but not functioning as a married couple. There may be short periods during this time where you have lived together, for example, an attempt at reconciliation.

However, as with desertion you will not be able to count these periods towards the two years separation. Therefore, if you have a trial reconciliation period for three months then you will have to wait two years and three months before you can apply for divorce.

The fundamental difference between desertion and separation with consent is that you would not be granted a divorce on the basis of separation if your spouse did not give his or her consent to the divorce.

The court has rigid criteria for proving that your spouse consents to the divorce. Consent is only seen as valid if your spouse has freely given it without pressure. There must also be full understanding on his or her part of what a divorce will mean and how it will affect his or her life.

The court sends a form to divorcing parties soon after initial divorce papers are filed, together with explanatory notes and it is at this point when your spouse will give consent. If your spouse will not consent to divorce and you cannot prove either desertion or adultery then you will be in the position where you will have to wait until five years separation has elapsed before you can seek a divorce. In relation to the above, i.e., divorces granted on the basis of two years separation and consent or five years separation, the courts can exercise special powers to ensure that the financial and personal position of the respondent is protected. The courts can sometimes delay the process of divorce, or even prevent it, to make sure that there is no undue suffering or exploitation.

Five years separation

The final of the "five facts" is the fact of five years separation. If you have been separated for five or more years the courts will grant a divorce whether or not the other party agrees to it, subject to what has been said above. Again, the courts will allow for a period of attempted reconciliation up to six months and the same rules concerning length of time apply as with the other facts. Should you live together for longer than six months, the courts will demand that you start the five-year period again.

Reconciliation

As been shown, in all the provisions of the law relating to each of the five facts which have to be demonstrated in addition to the main ground of "irretrievable breakdown", there are built in provisions for reconciliation. The law is fairly flexible when taking into account attempts at reconciling and sorting out differences.

In effect, these built in provisions allow for a period of up to six months in which both parties can make a concerted attempt at solving their problems. If these attempts are unsuccessful then their legal position vis-a-vis divorce proceedings will not be jeopardized. The reconciliation provisions apply for a period up to six months or separate periods not exceeding six months.

In addition to this, a solicitor, if you have one, will need to certify that he or she has discussed the possibility of reconciliation with you and has ensured that both parties know where to seek advice and guidance if they really wish to attempt reconciliation. The court, if it so wishes, can also adjourn proceedings to give both parties further time to decide whether they genuinely wish to make a further effort to prolong their marriage.

At the end of this book can be found names and addresses of various organizations which can help with the process of reconciliation. The best known of these is RELATE.

Alternative Dispute Resolution-conciliation and mediation services

There is a fundamental difference between reconciliation, and those services which offer help, and Alternative Dispute Resolution..

Conciliation is directed towards making parting easier to handle. The role of the conciliator is to sort out at least some of the difficulties between those who have made a definite and firm decision to obtain a divorce.

The process of conciliation can take place either out of court, or in court. In court, conciliation only arises once the process of litigating for divorce has commenced. It is particularly relevant where the future of children is under discussion.

With in-court conciliation, there is usually what is known as a "pre trial review" of the issues and problems which parties to a divorce are unable to settle themselves. Both the court welfare officer and the district judge are involved in this process.

Out of court conciliation and mediation is intended to assist both parties in reaching an agreement at a stage before they arrive in court, or approach the court. The person involved at this stage is usually always professionally trained, a social worker normally, and who will act as go between. Both parties can also use specially trained legal personnel, lawyers, to help them reach an agreement. This process is like the process of arbitration and is intended to make the formal legal proceedings less hostile and acrimonious. The Ministry of Justice provides details about mediation services local to you. In the next chapter, I will be dealing with the actual commencement of divorce proceedings following your decision to take action to end your marriage.

3

Commencing Proceedings

Using a solicitor

Although it makes sense to take legal advice when taking your first steps towards divorce, there is no rule that says you have to. Although this book is primarily about assisting a person to do their own divorce, it is important to examine the role of the solicitor, in the first instance, in order to get an idea of the advantages.

The amount of advice you will need from a solicitor will depend entirely on the circumstances of your case and the complexities involved. One of the reasons for reading a book such as this is to broaden your knowledge and put yourself in a stronger position to handle proceedings

Most divorces will have two fairly distinct stages - the first step of obtaining the divorce decree (divorce) and the more complicated problems of sorting out property and financial matters and making arrangements concerning children.

As with most county court procedures now, the procedure for commencing divorce and the subsequent steps up to the issuing of a decree is largely paperwork. Provided that the circumstances of your divorce are straightforward then there is no real need to consult a solicitor at all. In the next chapter, I will be discussing the actual procedure and how to obtain a divorce without a solicitor.

It is up to both parties to ascertain the complexity of the divorce before deciding to go it alone. The questions you should be asking yourselves, preferably during a face- to-face meeting, are whether or not the marriage can be ended with the minimum of problems.

If you are childless and there is no property at stake and there will be no financial complications then you should be able to proceed without a solicitor.

If, however, you own property and have children and also have life insurance policies and pension schemes etc, then you will need to try to reach agreement concerning the division of these. This is where divorce gets complicated and may entail you requesting legal advice.

The division of your assets is a matter for you but it has to be reached by agreement. I will be discussing financial matters and children later in the book.

One other aspect of do-it-yourself divorce is that it can be time consuming. Some people cannot spare the valuable time involved and will be happier to leave it to a solicitor.

A solicitor will handle the whole matter for you, when instructed, from obtaining initial information to obtaining a decree. Your main input will be to check over the necessary paperwork at each stage, as required and, in certain cases to deliver documents to the court. However, all of this will be done at the request and direction of the solicitor.

Your future arrangements

Whilst not essential to consult a solicitor, it is wise to at least get a view on future arrangements which you have negotiated. This is particularly important when it comes to future tax arrangements.

If it is necessary to ask a court to determine future arrangements, because of the inability of parties to a divorce to agree or negotiate, then a solicitor may need to take charge of the whole process, although not necessarily as the whole court process is designed to assist people to carry out their own divorce without legal help. Remember, the more a solicitor does for you the more it will cost. You should both bear this in mind when beginning discussions.

Your choice of solicitor

Not all solicitors deal with divorce cases, as this is a specialized area. In addition, not all solicitors operate the "Legal Help Scheme" (see below) which provides for legal aid.

It is always advisable for parties to a divorce to use separate solicitors over divorce. Solicitors, in the main, would prefer to represent one party and not both as this can present certain conflicts of loyalty and interest, particularly where there are antagonisms. The first task is for you to choose a solicitor. This can be done by either consulting business pages or, perhaps better, requesting a list of recommended solicitors from an advice agency, such as the Citizens Advice Bureau.

You may also feel that you will be eligible for legal help and you should ensure that the firm of solicitors that you choose operate this. Solicitors who do operate under legal help will be marked on the list of firms and solicitor's offices often clearly demonstrate their participation in the scheme by a sign showing two people sitting at a table with the words "legal aid" underneath.

When you have decided on a firm of solicitors, you should then contact them to make an initial appointment to discuss the matter. Your decision to allow a firm to act for you is a commercial one, and you will want in the initial stages to determine the costs and timeframe for your divorce. As there are a number of firms you should at first test the market in order to ensure that you are getting the best deal.

How much will it cost?

Although the costs of solicitors can be quite high, you should be able to keep the overall cost to a reasonable level.

With divorce costs and solicitors charges the first thing to know is that there are normally three possible legal issues involved in a divorce:

1) The divorce itself, obtaining the divorce and, more particularly the decree nisi-which enables both parties to remarry if they wish. The cost of divorce in this narrow sense is quite modest as it involves a distinct process, which can also be achieved oneself.
2) Issues involving the matrimonial property-basically deciding who gets what and whether any maintenance will be paid and so on. The technical phrase for this part of the process is 'ancillary relief'.
3) Issues involving children-access, contact, residence, maintenance etc.

It is the latter two areas that can prove to be quite costly.

If dealing with a straightforward divorce then the costs can, more or less, be fixed. Assuming that the divorce is uncontested, there is a court fee, currently 340 (2012) to issue a divorce petition which has to be paid to the court. There is also a court fee of 45 payable to obtain the decree absolute and, normally, there is an affidavit which needs to be sworn during the proceedings which costs approximately 7.50 in most cases. This means that total disbursements payable to the courts are in the region of 390. This cost is not cast in stone as there may be extra cost if, for example, the Respondent (person who received the divorce petition) does not reply and it may be necessary to arrange personal service. After the court fees comes the solicitor's charges, which can be around 400 plus VAT. This may vary and you will need to obtain quotes. Therefore, the cost of a basic divorce is around 850, once court fees have been taken into account.

Legal Help

Legal Help allows people with a low income to get free legal advice and help from a solicitor or an experienced legal adviser. The solicitor or adviser must have a contract with the Legal Services Commission (LSC) to be able to provide Legal Help.

What does Legal Help cover?

Legal Help covers all the help you might need from a solicitor or legal adviser in preparing a case to go to court. This may include getting general advice on any legal problems, It may also include your solicitor or adviser writing letters, negotiating, getting a barrister's opinion and preparing a written case for a tribunal. Legal Help could also cover the costs of mediation in non-family cases. Mediation is a way of negotiating, where the parties are helped by a neutral mediator to find a solution acceptable to them both.

Legal problems covered by Legal Help

Legal Help covers advice on general legal problems. In relation to divorce it will help with advice about:

- family law such as financial support after marriage or disputes about children. You could also get advice about undefended divorce or dissolution of a civil partnership

- the buying and selling of your home, but only if this is needed to carry out a court order or if it's the result of a divorce, legal separation or dissolved civil partnership

- a discrimination case, where you are treated unfairly because of age, disability, gender reassignment, marriage and civil partnership, pregnancy and maternity, race, religion or belief, sex or sexual orientation

- an adoption, but only if there's a dispute about adoption

To qualify for Legal Help, there are financial conditions - see below. If you meet the financial conditions, you'll normally get Legal Help for as long as the solicitor or adviser agrees there is 'sufficient benefit' in continuing with the case. 'Sufficient benefit' means that the case has to be one that has a chance of success. Also if it's a case where money is involved, there has to be a clear cost benefit to you. This is designed to weed out hopeless and non-legal matters. Once you've been granted Legal Help, your case will be regularly reviewed to make sure that these conditions continue to be met.

What are the financial conditions for Legal Help

Legal Help if you're getting benefits

You will get Legal Help if you or your partner receive:

- income support

- income-related Employment and Support Allowance

- income-based Jobseeker's Allowance

- guarantee credit part of Pension Credit.

If you don't get any of these benefits your income and capital will be looked at to see if you can get Legal Help.

Legal Help if you have income

If your gross monthly income is over £2,657 you won't get Legal Help. 'Gross income' means before tax and national insurance are taken off and it excludes certain social security benefits. If you have more than four children, this limit goes up by £222 for the fifth and each additional child. You have to include your partner's income unless your partner is the person who you are in dispute with.

If your gross monthly income is £2,657 or less, your solicitor or adviser will then check out what is your disposable income. 'Disposable income' is the amount of income you have left after deductions have been made for national insurance, child support and tax. Also, if you have a partner who isn't earning or if you have children, a certain amount of your income won't be taken into account. If your partner is earning, their income will be taken into account, unless your partner is the person who you are in dispute with.

To qualify for Legal Help, your disposable monthly income can't be more than £733. If you are within this limit, you don't have to pay anything towards Legal Help.

Legal Help if you have capital
If you have **disposable capital** (savings) of over £8,000, you won't get Legal Help. Disposable capital includes:

- money in the bank

- valuable items

- the value of your home (if you own it). This depends on how much the property is worth and how much your mortgage is.

You have to include your partner's capital unless your partner is the person who you are in dispute with.

If you're getting Income Support, income-related Employment and Support Allowance, income-based Jobseeker's Allowance or the guarantee credit part of Pension Credit, you'll automatically get Legal Help regardless of the value of your home or of any other capital you have.

More information about financial eligibility for Legal Help

For more information about whether you qualify for Legal Help, you can use the eligibility calculator on the Ministry of Justice website at www.justice.gov.uk.

How to apply for Legal Help

If you qualify for Legal Help, you'll need to see a solicitor, or an adviser with a contract to provide this type of legal aid. The solicitor or adviser will ask you to fill in an application form at the start of the interview. They will use the information you give on the form to decide whether you qualify.

Family Help

If you have a serious family dispute, you may be entitled to Family Help. Family Help helps you to sort out your dispute. This could be through negotiation or some other means. Family Help covers all forms of legal help or representation other than representation at a defended final court hearing or appeal.

It can also cover help with mediation in a family dispute, for example, it can help you draw up the agreement you reached with the other party in the dispute.

In most cases, you must meet certain financial conditions to qualify for Family Help. These are the same as for Legal Help. If you're a parent, expectant parent or person with parental responsibility, you don't have to meet these financial qualifications to qualify for advice where the local authority is intending to start care or supervision proceedings.

Family Mediation

If you are involved in a family dispute, for example, about contact with your children after your relationship has broken down, you might find it helpful to go to mediation. This is where an independent mediator helps you to reach an agreement without you needing to go to court. The mediator does not make any decisions for you but helps you and the other party to make your own decisions. If you decide to go to mediation, you may be able to get help under Family mediation to pay for the mediator. You must meet certain financial conditions. These are the same for Legal Help

Community Legal Advice helpline

If you live on a low income or get benefits, you may be able to get help from the Community Legal Advice helpline. The Community Legal Advice helpline can give you free, independent and confidential advice about:

- education

- benefits and tax credits

- employment

- housing

- debt

- family.

The helpline number is: 0845 345 4345. It is open from 9am to 8pm, Monday to Friday and from 9am to 12.30pm on a Saturday. Calls cost no more than 4p a minute from a BT landline. Calls from mobiles are usually more. If you're worried about the cost of the phone-call, you can ask an adviser to call you back. You can text 'legalaid' and your name to 80010 and an adviser will call you back within 24 hours.

The helpline has a translation service if you would like advice in a language other than English or Welsh.

There is also a minicom service for people who are deaf, hard-of-hearing or speech-impaired and a type-talk service for people with hearing difficulties.

Help with Mediation

Help with Mediation has its own special rules. It is available only if you are taking part in family mediation or you have successfully reached an agreement with your spouse and need legal advice or support from a solicitor. For example, you may need a solicitor to put your agreement into a legal form so that it can be submitted to the court.

Recovering the cost of divorce from your spouse

It is wise to agree between you beforehand who pays what costs towards the divorce. One of the fundamental principles when handling divorce is to try to sort as much out as possible in order to minimize future complications and also costs, both emotional and financial.

If you cannot decide, or agree, the court will take a view as to who should bear costs. As a general rule, the petitioner will hardly ever be ordered to pay the respondents costs of divorce. A respondent, however, may have to pay a petitioners costs, although not if the petitioner is eligible under the Legal Help Scheme. This depends entirely on the basis for divorce. You can change your solicitor at any point in time if you are unhappy and are paying for the service out of your own pocket. However, you will have to finalize your solicitors bill up to that point. If you feel that you have a complaint then you can complain to the Solicitors Complaints Bureau, set up by the Law Society as part of its regulatory functions. Again, any advice agency will give you details concerning this agency, and how to go about complaining.

If you are receiving benefits under the Legal Help Scheme then your right to change solicitors may be more complicated. However, if you are very dissatisfied then you will usually be able to change solicitors. You should find another solicitor and explain the circumstances. He or she will then arrange to take your case on.

Although I have mentioned it previously, it is essential that you sort as many problems out as possible before consulting a solicitor. The more you know and the less problematic the divorce is likely to be then the less the cost to you, particularly if you are meeting it out of your own pocket.

In addition, the clearer the picture when you do eventually commence divorce proceedings the smoother the transition to obtaining your decree will be.

In the next chapter I will be describing the steps towards obtaining a divorce and how to do-it-yourself. As stated, it is a question of paperwork and procedure and, if arrangements are not too complicated then there is every reason why you can obtain your own divorce without the unnecessary involvement of a solicitor.

4

The Procedure for Obtaining a Divorce

In undefended petitions, both spouses accept that the divorce will go ahead. In defended petitions, one party is filing a defence against the petition.

A special procedure was introduced to deal with undefended divorce petitions, primarily because of the large volume of cases presented to the courts.

At present, there is a set pattern, which you must follow if you wish to obtain a divorce:

a) the petition must be filled in (form D8-see appendix)

b) the petition must enclose a statement of arrangements for the children (if appropriate)

c) three copies of the petition(s) must be sent to the registrar of the divorce county court.

d) there must be sufficient copies for the other parties to the divorce (3)

e) the respondent will then receive his or her copies from the court.

f) other parties involved will receive their copies.

g) the respondent must, on a prescribed form (D10) acknowledge service.

h) the respondent must make clear that he or she has no intention to defend.

i) the documents are examined by a court official (the divorce registrar)

j) the divorce registrar then certifies that the facts of the case are approved.

k) the judge pronounces the decree nisi in open court.

l) the decree is made absolute on application by the petitioner.

Each of the above steps will be discussed briefly below.

The preparation of the divorce petition.

Either you or your solicitor will prepare the divorce petition. The forms used to commence a divorce can all be obtained from the county court local to you. In addition, they can be obtained from the internet (Her Majesty's Courts and Tribunals Service) or from a Citizens Advice Bureau. As discussed in solicitor's costs there is a fee to commence divorce. The website will provide information concerning fees or this can be obtained from your local county court (divorce court).

On this form you will record details of your marriage and your children and the grounds on which you are seeking a divorce. You will also list the claims that you are asking the court to consider. This part is particularly important. For example you may wish the court to consider financial matters for you.

Normally, you would include your address on the form but you can make application to the court to leave out your address if this poses any danger to you.

It is of the utmost importance that you take care at this stage because you are asking the court to make a very important decision on the basis of information given. You should avoid exaggerating the truth.

The statement of arrangements

If there are children involved you must fill in another document known simply as "statement of arrangements for children" (form D8A). This sets out the arrangements you intend to make for children once the divorce is granted.

A child, for the purposes of the court is any child who is a child of both parties, an adopted child, or any other child who has been treated by both as part of your family. This does not include children boarded out by local authorities or social services or other voluntary organizations.

Although the courts are not generally concerned with the welfare of adult children (over 16) you will be required to give details of children under 18 who are still receiving instruction at an educational establishment or undergoing other training such as for trade or profession.

The information required for the statement of arrangements will be:

a) where the children will live after divorce

b) who else will be residing there

c) who will look after them

d) where they are to be educated

e) what financial arrangements have been proposed for them

f) what arrangements have been made for the other parent to see them

g) whether they have any illness or disability

i) whether they are under the care or supervision of a person or organization (i.e. social services)

When you have completed this form your spouse should be in agreement. If she or he is not then there will be an opportunity at a later stage to make alternative proposals to the court.

Serving the papers on the respondent and the co-respondent

Once the petition has been received by the courts the court office will then send a copy, plus copy of statement of arrangements to the respondent. This is known as "serving" the documents on the respondent. He or she will also receive two other documents from the court-the "acknowledgement of service" (D10) and the "notice of proceedings".

The notice of proceedings informs the respondent that divorce proceedings have been commenced against him or her and that person must acknowledge service within eight days. There are further instructions concerning seeking legal help or filling in acknowledgement personally.

This document, the acknowledgement of service, is self-explanatory and is designed in question and answer form. It is designed to ensure the court that the respondent has received the papers and is fully aware of impending divorce proceedings against them. The court will not proceed with the case until it has received this information.

If you have commenced proceedings on the ground of adultery then the third party, who is known as the co-respondent, is entitled to be notified of the divorce proceedings.

Non-defence of divorce proceedings

Where the respondent does not wish to defend proceedings, the next steps should be quite straightforward. The court will send either you or your solicitor a copy of the completed acknowledgement of service together with copies of two more forms known as "request for directions for trial" (special procedure) and the "affidavit of evidence" (special procedure) The special procedure indicates that the divorce process will be streamlined. Before, all petitioners seeking a divorce had to go to court and give evidence before a judge. This is no longer necessary. Like many county court procedures the route is now simplified and quicker.

The affidavit of evidence, like all affidavits, confirms that what you have said in your petition is true. You will need to "take an oath" in front of a solicitor which is called "swearing" the affidavit. Any questions concerning the truth later could ultimately, if it is discovered that you have lied, lead to contempt of court.

The "request for directions for trial" is a basic form requesting the court to proceed with your case. Both documents, the affidavit and the request for directions are then returned to court.

The case is then examined by an official of the court who will either declare that the facts of the case are proven, or otherwise.

If the district judge is happy with the case he or she will issue a certificate that you are entitled to a decree of divorce. Any claims for costs will also be considered at this stage.

When a certificate has been issued, a date will be fixed for decree nisi to be pronounced in open court by judge or district judge. You will be informed of this date but you need not attend court. However, if there is a dispute over costs you will need to attend and the matter will be dealt with by the judge Both the respondent and petitioner are then sent a copy of the decree nisi by the court. However, you have not yet reached the stage of being finally divorced. It is only when your divorce has been made absolute at a later stage that you will be free to remarry if you wish. A decree absolute follows approximately six weeks after decree nisi. If the district judge is not satisfied that you should be granted a divorce, then you will either be asked to produce further evidence or the matter will be sent for trial.

You may be entitled to legal aid if this happens. This is dependent on your income and you should seek advice. If you are refused a divorce, and you have been handling the case yourself then you will most certainly need to go and see a solicitor.

Defence of divorce

If the respondent or co-respondent has returned the papers stating that he or she intends to defend the petition, your next move will be very much dependent on whether an "answer" setting out the defence has been filed. The respondent has 29 days to file a reply.

If a defence has been filed, then the special procedure designed to speed up the process can no longer be used. In this case it is advisable to see a solicitor. There will eventually be a date given for a hearing in court at which both the petitioner and respondent will be expected to attend.

Evidence will be given to the judge who will then have to decide if a divorce should be granted. Legal aid would almost certainly be available and the whole process, depending on the defence can be quite lengthy.

If you are the respondent and you feel that you wish to defend the petition you will almost certainly need to see a solicitor and take advice.

In general, undefended straightforward cases, particularly where there are no children involved, can be done on a do-it-yourself basis. Anything more complicated will mean that you will probably need to see a solicitor.

If any other problems arise, such as the respondent either failing or refusing to return acknowledgement of service, proceedings will be delayed whilst a visit by a court official is made. This visit is to ascertain and provide evidence of service. If the respondent cannot be traced, a request can be made to the court for the petition to be heard anyway. Again, this will result in delay.

5

Children and Divorce

When considering a divorce petition, it is the duty of a court to have regard to all of the circumstances within that petition.

The first, and possibly most important consideration will be the welfare of any children in a family, under the age of eighteen years old.

Whereas the practice of the courts prior to 1989 was to make orders regulating where the children of a divorced family were to live (known as a Custody Order) and what contact each parent would have with that child (Access Order), the Children Act of 1989 (as amended by the Family Law Act 1996) has changed all of this.

The Children Act 1989

The underlying aim, or intention, of the Children Act of 1989 (as amended) is that, where there is marital breakdown the law should play as small a role as possible. Parents must continue to care for and to have responsibility for their children until they reach the age of 18.

As far as possible, when divorce proceedings are in process, parents should make their own decisions concerning a child's welfare. Therefore, the new Act seeks to minimize the courts role in final decisions.

However, should you decide to seek assistance from the courts, the Children Act of 1989 provides a range of orders, which can, if necessary, be used to resolve issues relating to children. The old Custody and Access orders have been replaced by four main types of order. The terms used are felt to be more appropriate:

1. *Residence orders*: these orders settle the arrangements as to where a child will live. Although this will normally be with one of the parents, third parties, such as relatives can apply for a residence order.

2. *Contact orders.* These regulate the contact that child will have with the person named in the order.

3. *Prohibited steps order.* This prohibits a parent from exercising his/her parental responsibility for a child in whatever way is stipulated in the order, i.e., a parent could be prohibited from bringing a child into contact with an undesirable person named in the order.

4. *Specific issue order.* This decides a particular issue which has arisen in connection with any aspect of parental responsibility for a child. One example could be where a child is to be educated.

It should be noted that a court has the power to make an order under the Children Act wherever one is necessary, whether or not divorce proceedings have commenced. If a petition for divorce has already been filed, the county court will almost certainly deal with the application. In other situations however, an application can be made to a magistrate's court instead. Because the Children Act of 1989 (as amended) has fundamentally changed the way the courts view the responsibility for children's welfare following divorce, it is necessary to look in a little more detail at the various orders.

Residence orders
If you and your spouse can reach agreement concerning where a child will live after the divorce, then the courts will not intervene. If however you cannot reach agreement then a residence order will be made.

Whatever the residence order stipulates however, you will both continue to have parental responsibility for the children. Although the parent with whom the child lives will go on making day to day decisions for the child, the other parent has a right to participate in more fundamental decisions such as education etc. If disagreement arises over these matters, one or other of the parents can seek a specific issue order or a prohibited steps order.

The most common type of residence order is for children to live with one parent and see the other parent regularly, for purposes of contact.

The most usual situation is for the mother to be the parent and for the father to have regular contact. A residence order can be made in favour of more than one person where the circumstances warrant it. For example, a residence order can be granted to a woman and new spouse.

If there are problems in issuing residence orders in the beginning, a court can issue a temporary order to regulate the situation, known as an interim order. This is rare, but the courts do have the powers.

The procedure for a residence order

Again, as with most county court procedures, the first step in applying for a residence order is to fill in the appropriate form setting out details about yourself and also details concerning the type of order you are seeking.

This form is then served on the other parent who will file it with the court and serve on you a brief answer as to the proposals. The court will give directions as to how the matter will proceed. If you have any witnesses supporting your case for the order, it is highly likely that you will have to inform them that they may have to attend court to give evidence. If you have a solicitor acting for you then that person will request details. It is likely that if matters start to become complicated then you will be using a solicitor.

The court will usually also seek an independent report about your case to help it reach a decision. This would be prepared by a welfare officer or some other agency experienced in these matters.

The solicitor representing you will ask for a copy before the hearing of your case in order to ensure that you agree with the contents.

After the court has received all the evidence it needs and you have attended court, the order that the judge makes is usually intended to be long term. However, a residence order is never absolutely final (it can't be) and can be altered if circumstances make this necessary.

One fundamental principle guiding any judge's decision is that the welfare of the child must come first.

When a residence order has been made and is in force, the law provides that no person shall be allowed to change the surname of that child without the consent of everyone with parental responsibility, or leave of the court.

If the other parent will not consent to a change of name then you will have to make an application to the court and convince the judge that there is good reason to change the name.

If you wish to take your child abroad, and a residence order has been made then the written consent of every person with parental responsibility is needed, or leave of the court. The only exception to his rule is that the person in whose favour an order has been made can take the child abroad for less than one month.

Contact orders

The court will expect both parties to agree as to what is reasonable contact in your own particular case. If you can't reach agreement the court will decide what is reasonable in your case and will define when contact should take place.

The court will take a fairly stringent view concerning contact and will, if there is strong evidence that it is not in the interests of a child, ensure that contact is prevented. However, the court will only do this in quite exceptional circumstances. Normally, notwithstanding the emotions surrounding applications to restrict contact, the court will act in the best interests of the child.

If you are making application for the child to stay overnight with the contact parent, the court will only agree if suitable accommodation is provided. If the child genuinely does not wish to stay overnight then a court is unlikely to make such an order.

If the court is worried about arrangements for contact then it can sometimes arrange for supervised contact visits, to make sure that everything is all right. If this proves to be the case then supervision will cease.

Some areas have family centres where contact visits can take place with family centre workers while waiting to assist transfer of the child from one parent to another, to ensure that problems do not arise.

Like a residence order, a contact order is never final. This is because individual circumstances change and you may need to ask the court to reconsider the order and the provisions made.

It is obviously much easier if both parents agree on the nature of contact, avoiding the need for an order. You should think very carefully about the arrangements and take into account days such as birthdays, Christmas day etc. It is during these times that each parent will want contact and you should try to agree on a framework, which will minimize possibilities of emotional upset.

6

Financial Support
For Children-The Child Support Agency

About child maintenance

Child maintenance is financial support towards a child's everyday living costs. Separated parents can arrange child maintenance between themselves by making a family-based arrangement. They can also ask the CSA or courts to get involved.

What child maintenance is

Child maintenance is usually regular, reliable financial support that helps towards a child's everyday living costs.

The parent who doesn't have main day-to-day care of the child pays child maintenance to the parent or person who does have main day-to-day care. The person with care can be a grandparent or guardian.

But child maintenance can be about more than just money. It's about parents taking responsibility for their children, even if they live apart from them. It can make a big difference to a child's well-being, because it can help create a more stable environment for them.

Arranging child maintenance

All separated parents can arrange child maintenance between themselves if they both agree to it. This is called a family-based arrangement.

Where this is not possible, parents can ask the Child Support Agency (CSA) or the courts to get involved.

Family based arrangements

If you and the other parent want to, you can make a family-based arrangement. This is when you arrange child maintenance between yourselves.

It's often the quickest and easiest way of arranging child maintenance because there's little paperwork to do.

A family-based arrangement means you can:

- agree between yourselves how much child maintenance payments should be, and when they should be made

- agree to change your arrangement if either parent's circumstances change

- pay for or receive things like clothing for your child instead of money, if you both agree to it

This type of arrangement isn't usually legally binding. This means that no-one will be able to collect any missed payments or enforce broken agreements. However, if it breaks down, either parent can ask the CSA or courts to arrange child maintenance at any time.

There are lots of tools available, on the DirectGov website to help you set up a family-based arrangement, like a:

- child maintenance calculator to help you agree on an amount

- discussion guide to help you talk things through with the other parent

- family-based arrangement form which you can use to keep a record of what you agree

You can also ask a professional mediator to help you if you want to.

CSA arrangements

Sometimes parents can't sort out child maintenance between themselves so a family-based arrangement is not possible. In some circumstances it's not suitable, for example if there is a risk of violence or abuse. In such cases, the CSA will work out a child maintenance amount. It can also arrange for child maintenance to be collected from one parent and then passed on to the other parent.

Court orders

Parents can also arrange child maintenance and enforce payments through the courts. This is done using a Consent Order in England and Wales, and a Minute of Agreement in Scotland.

Usually child maintenance is arranged this way if parents are already going to court for another reason – for example, if they are getting a divorce. Using the courts to arrange child maintenance can be expensive. Legal Aid won't cover the costs if you are only going to court to arrange child maintenance.

You can find more information about court orders for child maintenance on the Child Maintenance Options website.

Child maintenance and benefits

Since October 2008, all parents have been able to choose how to arrange child maintenance, even if they're on benefits.

Also, since April 2010 parents with care can keep all child maintenance paid to them and this should no longer affect their income-related benefits.

More help with child maintenance

The Child Maintenance Options service provides both parents with information about:

- family-based arrangements

- other options for arranging child maintenance

- other issues affecting separated families

This service is free to use.

Using the CSA to arrange child maintenance

The CSA runs the current statutory child maintenance schemes. If you or the other parent opens a CSA case, it will work out how much child maintenance should be paid. It can also collect and pass on child maintenance payments. Find out about using the CSA, including how to apply.

Who is eligible to use the CSA?
You can apply to the Child Support Agency (CSA) if you are a:

- parent with care

- non-resident parent

- grandparent or other guardian of the children needing child maintenance

- child living in Scotland

The parent or person with care is the parent or carer who the child normally lives with. The non-resident parent is the parent who the child does not normally live with.

The CSA can't accept applications if the parent with care or the children live outside of the UK.

It also can't accept applications if the non-resident parent lives outside of the UK, unless they:

- work for a UK-based employer

- work for the civil service

- work for a 'prescribed body', for example the NHS

- are in the armed forces

In addition, the CSA can't accept applications when certain child maintenance agreements are already in place. This includes:

- court orders covering child maintenance that were made before 3 March 2003

- court orders covering child maintenance which are less than 12 months old

- written maintenance agreements made before 5 April 1993

If you want to change one of the above arrangements you need to ask the court that made the arrangement.

What the CSA can help you with

If you decide to use the CSA it can help you to:

- try to find the other parent if you don't know where they live

- help to sort out any disagreements about parentage

- work out how much child maintenance should be paid

Once your case has been opened, the CSA can:

- arrange for non-resident parents to pay child maintenance

- pass payments on to the parent with care

- look again at your child maintenance payments when changes in parents' circumstances are reported

- take action if payments are not made

Applying to use the CSA

You can apply to use the CSA using the following link.

- Applying to use the CSA

If you live in Northern Ireland, you should apply to the Child Maintenance and Enforcement Division (CMED). You can get more information about CMED on the NI Direct website.

How long it takes to arrange child maintenance

The CSA aims to get child maintenance payments to parents with care as soon as possible. In most cases a payment should be made to parent's with care within six weeks of the CSA making an arrangement with the non-resident parent.

How the CSA works out child maintenance

To work out child maintenance amounts, the CSA uses information about the non-resident parent's circumstances. This information includes:

- the non-resident parent's income

- the number of children they need to pay child maintenance for

- how often the child or children stays overnight with them

- the number of other children the non-resident parent (or their partner) gets child benefit for

Contacting the Child Support Agency

There are several ways to contact the Child Support Agency (CSA).

If you have a general question about child maintenance

If you have a general question about child maintenance, you can contact the Child Maintenance Options service. For contact details use the below address.

www.cmoptions.org

If you have a general enquiry about the CSA

There are several ways you can contact the CSA if you want to make a general enquiry.

You can call the National helpline.

- **National helpline: 08457 133 133**

You can also send a fax.

- **Fax: 08457 138 924**

If you have speech or hearing difficulties you can use the CSA's textphone service.

- **Textphone: 08457 138 924**

If you want to write to the CSA, use the following address:

Child Support Agency
National Helpline
PO Box 55
Brierley Hill
DY5 1YL

If you want to apply to the CSA

For information about applying to the CSA, use the address below.

*   www.direct.gov.uk/csaapply

7

Financial Arrangements and Divorce

Family assets

When a marriage breaks down, everything which has been earned or owned during the marriage is considered part of the assets of that marriage. On divorce these assets can all be redistributed no matter who earned them during the marriage period. As the emphasis is on family assets, property owned by either spouse before the marriage cannot be counted.

However, if one spouse buys a house, or acquires some other asset, before marrying, with a view to living in it or using it together, then this will be counted as an asset.

When a divorce takes place, usually the couple concerned will decide between them what should happen to family assets, the most significant usually being the house, unless there is a large sum of money involved.

If an agreement cannot be reached concerning the division of assets then the couple can ask the court to decide who is to have what. The court has very wide powers to redistribute the family assets. Its task is to try to reach a fair and just division in all the circumstances of each case. The duty of husband and wife to support each other does not end on divorce. In principle, the duty to maintain remains. There have been a number of challenges to this principal however.

In particular, the court must consider whether it would not be desirable to impose a clean break on the couple. This is seen as an alternative to long-term support. It is obligatory for the courts to consider the question of ending one spouse's financial dependence on the other, once the marriage itself has come to an end. The main difficulties in making a judgement of this kind is that circumstances will vary so much from one couple to another. The main guidelines for the court are:

- ·How long the couple have been married

- ·How old the parties to marriage are

- ·Whether there are any children involved

If a marriage has been short lived, the parties to it are young and there are no children involved then the courts would almost certainly want to see a clean break.

The one-third rule

In general, if a clean break from marriage is not ordered, then the court calculates on the basis of the "one third" rule. Using this formula the wife gets one third of the combined income-exclusive of maintenance for the children. This is not a rigid rule but the basis for starting calculations in each case.

Factors taken into account by the court when making an order

The court will look at income of each partner, earning capacity, property and other financial resources. This amounts, usually, to the total family resources and is what the court will look at beyond what is said by the parties.

Other matters taken into account by a court would be expectations under a will or other family settlement.

The court will also look at financial needs, obligations and responsibilities, both now and in the near future. This covers all out goings such as food, clothing and other essential items. If either spouse has set up home with another partner or intends to remarry, then that second families needs will also be an important factor in the equation.

Parties to a marriage are not expected to be in the position that they would have been if the marriage had survived. However, in the case of wealthy or very wealthy households adjustments are sometimes made to compensate for loss of standards.

A court will take into account how old parties to a marriage are. A younger person may need less support than an elderly one. If either spouse suffers from a disability or serious illness, this will obviously be a factor in assessing the division of assets.

Pension rights -The 1995 Pensions Act

Under the pensions Act 1995, which covers petitions filed since 1st July 1996, courts must now take pension rights into account. They have the power to redistribute other assets as compensation for loss of pension rights or to order pension trustees or managers to 'earmark' part of the pension to be paid at retirement to the ex-wife, in other words to allocate a share of the husbands pension to the wife in the future (and any tax free cash he takes at retirement).

The husband can also make a parallel application for his wife's pension to be earmarked in his favour. The part that is earmarked can either be a percentage of the whole pension or a fixed sum.

Pension sharing

For divorce proceedings started on or after 1st December 2000, (following the introduction of the Welfare Reform and Pensions Act 1999) the courts have a further option: pension sharing (formerly called pension splitting). Unlike earmarking, pension sharing is likely to be a popular option. Under pension sharing, the value of a husbands pension rights is calculated. Part of that value is then transferred to the wife to fund her own pension. The values of the husbands rights is reduced by the sum transferred.

The question of pension rights following divorce is fraught with problems and was changed significantly by the 1995 Pensions act. Pensions almost always represent a considerable aspect of family investment in the long term. For a couple who divorce late in life, the loss of pension rights can mean a considerable loss of future material comfort.

A woman can also lose the prospect of a widow's pension once she is divorced. There are two considerations for a judge when considering pension rights:

Set off

This permits the division of the matrimonial assets to compensate the wife for any loss of pension rights of the husband that she would have had if she had remained married to him.

Earmarking

This allows a judge to direct that a part of the pension lump sum that would come into being on retirement, to the wife. Before there can be any transfer there must be a valuation of the pension.

Protection of assets

If there is manoeuvring before the divorce is finalized, for example one spouse attempting to engineer the division of assets to his or her favour, then there are a series of steps which divorcing couple should be aware of which can prevent this happening.

The Home

This is usually the most significant asset at stake and it is essential to ensure that this is not sold or otherwise disposed of without your knowledge.

If your name is on the title deeds of the property then it cannot be sold without your knowledge or consent. However, if you are uncertain of this then it is absolutely essential that you consult a solicitor and ensure that you can register a land charge or notice on the property.

This notice would ensure that any would be purchaser is fully aware of your right to live in the property. If the property was purchased then the person buying would have to let you continue living there.

Protection from the courts generally

If you can satisfy the courts that you have a claim to a share of the family assets or income and that your spouse is about to make off with some of your assets, or already has done so, the court can prevent this taking place.

If you are seriously worried that this will be the case then you should contact your solicitor immediately. It is easier to act before anything takes place than afterwards.

A court can make an injunction to prevent your spouse from disposing of any of the family assets. If he or she does not obey this injunction then imprisonment can follow. The court could also make an order that your spouse pay over money to an independent person for safe keeping, such as a court account or bank account.

If you find out that your spouse has got rid of assets after the event, the process of reclaiming is that much harder. The court has the power to set transactions aside, only provided that they were not made with someone who has paid a proper price and was ignorant of the circumstances.

An example could be shares in a company. If the disposal was to general purchasers, then the ability of the court to get back those stocks is very limited. However, if another party was involved, such as a relative, and the disposal, to that person, was in full knowledge of the circumstances then the courts job is that much easier

Obtaining financial help before divorce is finalised

In the early stages of the divorce, you will usually have to rely on your own savings or earnings until a settlement can be reached. Usually, it is the woman who is hardest hit and this section will assume that it is the woman who is seeking help.

Sooner or later, however, you will need more concrete assistance and there are two ways of obtaining this: by applying to the court for an order obliging your husband to maintain you and by applying for welfare benefits.

State and other benefits

There are various benefits available. There is a booklet, at the time of writing, called "Which Benefit"; this can be obtained from your local social security office. This booklet gives up to date information on the type of benefits currently available and your eligibility

There are a number of other leaflets available from other sources. The Child Poverty Action Group, for example, publish several guides and a regular information bulletin about benefits.

If you are in financial difficulty whilst still living with your spouse, you should seek advice about entitlement to benefits from a Citizens Advice Bureau or from your local social security office. There are situations, for example, where you can arrange to have your husband's income support to be paid to you instead of him, if he is refusing to support you and the children properly.

Type of help available once divorce proceedings have commenced

The divorce court can order a spouse to make regular cash payments to another to provide for needs until the divorce comes through. This is known as "maintenance pending suit", or maintenance until the divorce is decided (Ancillary Relief).

The court cannot order a spouse to make more substantial payments or divide assets until divorce has been granted. The court can, however, make an order as to who lives in the house until divorce, if the breakdown means that you cannot live under the same roof together.

The court can also take steps to prevent either of you from disposing of any of your property before it has taken the opportunity to consider what should be done with it in the future, if it feels that the disposal will affect future equal and fair distribution.

You can apply for a court order at any stage between the commencement of proceedings and the date on which decree nisi of divorce is made absolute, whether or not you are living apart.

If an order is made, maintenance pending suit, this will tide you over until longer-term plans can be made. Therefore, maintenance pending suit ceases to be payable when your divorce is made absolute.

However, if when your divorce has been finalized an order still has not been made then a maintenance pending suit order can be replaced by an "interim periodical order" which lasts until a final order is made.

When looking at the circumstances of your case in order to be able to make a maintenance pending suit order, the judge will look at the circumstances of both parties and concentrate on achieving a fair balance between what you need and what your spouse can pay. You will both be expected to provide details of your income from all sources and your regular expenses. Assessing your income and expenses may not always be that straightforward. For example, Social Security Benefits may vary depending on whether or not you receive maintenance.

You may have formed a relationship with another person. The fact that you have committed adultery will not normally prevent you receiving maintenance from your spouse. However, if you are living with another person, that person will probably help you to pay for your everyday needs. If this is the case, then maintenance will be reduced.

A good guide to whether or not you are entitled to maintenance pending suit is to draw up a chart which indicates whether or not your income exceeds your outgoings. If you earn more than you spend you are unlikely to get maintenance. If neither of you have commenced divorce proceedings then you will not be able to apply for maintenance. There are, however, other ways in which you can obtain assistance from the courts. The magistrates court can, for example, make various orders to provide maintenance.

The first requirement for an order like this is to demonstrate that you are eligible for such an order.

If you have not yet commenced divorce proceedings

If you have not yet commenced divorce proceedings, you will not be able to apply to the divorce court for maintenance pending suit. However, there are other ways in which you can obtain assistance from the courts.

The magistrates court

In order to obtain help with your financial situation from a magistrate's court, you must be able to show that you are eligible for a magistrate's court order. The following sets out the ways in which you can qualify for an order and the type of order that can be made. If you can prove that:

- Your husband has deserted you

- Your husband has behaved unreasonably
- Your husband has failed to provide reasonable maintenance for you
- Your husband has failed to provide or make reasonable contributions towards the maintenance of a child of the family.

You can then expect to obtain an order for maintenance payable to you at regular intervals and/or a lump sum payment of not more than £1000. If you and your husband have come to a financial arrangement that you would both like the court to put into an order, then the court can grant maintenance for yourself that you have agreed. If you and your husband have been separated by agreement for more than three months and your husband has been making maintenance payments to you and you would like the additional security of an order then a court can grant this order, subject to certain restrictions. Magistrates will decide on a sum to be paid by taking into account your needs and how much your husband can afford to pay.

If you are still living together

If you are living together when you apply to the magistrate's court, you can still obtain an order from the court. However, if you go on living together for a continuous period of more than six months after the order is made, an order for maintenance will cease to be effective.

If you are living apart when you get an order, but you subsequently start to live together again your maintenance order will cease if you live together for a continuous period of more than six months.

8

Protection in Your Home During and Following Divorce

If you are fortunate, you and your spouse may be able to part without animosity when you realize that your marriage is over. However, it is just as likely that you will have to remain under the same roof even though your personal relationships may be tense and strained. In many cases, when your marriage starts to break down, both of you will try to torment the other, to a degree not seen during happier times.

There are many things to consider if relationships start to deteriorate. If you have children the considerations will become more urgent. One of the main considerations will be that of: who moves out? Who takes care of the children, how will you get them to school and so on.

The courts are able to help considerably with these sorts of problems, and this chapter outlines the various powers of the court to help you until matters are sorted out.

How to get help from the courts
Help is available either from the county court or the magistrates court. Both husband and wife are equally entitled to help from the court, although it is more usual for the wife to seek help. In some cases, it may be more appropriate for each of you to ask the court to intervene in some way.

It is not necessary for either of you to have started divorce proceedings before you apply, nor essential that you are still living together. Neither does it matter who owns the house or whose name it is in.

Help from the magistrate's court

The magistrate's court can make orders protecting you or a child of the family from your spouse. These are called "personal protection orders". Before you can get a personal protection order, you will have to satisfy the court of the following:

- that your spouse has used violence or threatened to use violence against you and a child of the family and;
- that you need to be protected from him/her by an order of the court;

If you can satisfy these conditions, the court can make an order preventing your spouse from using or threatening violence against you and/or your family.

The magistrate's court can also make an order excluding your spouse from your home. This is called an "exclusion order". The magistrates will only make an exclusion order if your case is serious.

If your spouse has already been violent towards you or a child of the family, you must be able to show that you or the child are in danger of being physically injured by him/her, or would be if he were to be allowed into the home.

If your spouse has not actually been violent towards you or a child yet, you will have to demonstrate;

- that you or a child are in danger of being physically injured by him/her and;

- that he/she has threatened you or a child with violence and by doing so he was breaking an existing personal protection order already in force, or alternatively, that he/she has threatened you or a child with violence, and he/she has already demonstrated that they are capable of violent behaviour by using violence on someone else.

If necessary, when it makes an exclusion order the court can also order your spouse to allow you to return to live in the home. This might be appropriate, for example, if there was a serious risk that your spouse would move out as directed but at the same time change all the locks so that you could not get back into the property.

Help from the county court

There is a wide range of orders available from the county court. They fall into two categories; "non-molestation orders" and "exclusion orders". The technical name for an order of either type is an injunction. The 1996 Family Law Act has strengthened these provisions.

Non-molestation injunctions

The court can make an order prohibiting your spouse from molesting you or your children. This order is roughly the equivalent of the magistrate's personal protection order, although the county court is able to protect you not only from violence but from a wider range of behaviour on the part of your spouse.

Exclusion injunctions

The court can exclude your spouse from the family home and even from the immediate vicinity of the house and can also order him/her to permit you to return to live there if he/she has turned you out, or is preventing you from entering.

The court will not make this sort of order lightly. It must be fair, just and reasonable to do so. There are many factors to be taken into account including the behaviour of each of you, and both your personal circumstances. For instance, what, if any, alternative accommodation you would each be able to find if you had to leave, whether either of you will suffer injury to your physical or mental health if you have to go on living in the same house, and so on.

If you have children, the court will concentrate particularly on how the situation is affecting them. It will want to know how much it is distressing the children to see the relationship between you and your spouse deteriorate, what effect it would have on them if your spouse was ordered to leave and how they would be affected if he/she was to stay; whether they are, in fact, being directly involved in the breakdown of your marriage, perhaps because your spouse has threatened violence towards them.

When the court has all the information necessary, it is likely to approach its decision on the house in two parts. It will first decide whether the situation has got so bad that you can no longer go on living together as a family in the same house. If it considers that this is so, it has then got to decide how things can be arranged so that you and your spouse do not come into contact any more than is necessary.

If your house is small then the court may have no choice but to order you both out. If you have more room, it may be possible for the court to divide up the house and allocate part to each of you so you both have separate space.

If you have children, the courts decision will usually be determined by what is going to happen to the children. The parent who is going to look after them will normally be allowed to stay in the house while the other will have to move out. If there are no children, the court will decide what should be done by looking at the way you have both behaved and assessing which of you would be better able to fend for yourself if turned out of your home. If one of you has obviously behaved far more unreasonably than the other, that person can usually expect to be the one asked or ordered to leave.

If there is a serious possibility of your spouse making a nuisance of him/her self in the vicinity of the house at any time after he/she has been ordered to leave, the court can be asked to make a further order prohibiting him/her from coming within a specified distance of the house.

As with a non-molestation injunction, it is worth remembering that an exclusion injunction will not be granted unless there is real reason.

If you are asking the court for such an order you will have to attend court to give evidence about your circumstances, and you may also have to swear an affidavit setting out in writing why you need the courts help. Your spouse will also usually have the opportunity to give evidence at the court hearing.

It is up to the court to decide how long its order should last. It will generally specify the duration of the order when it makes it

Personal protection orders and non-molestation injunctions will generally last until you are divorced although the court can grant an injunction for a shorter or longer period. Exclusion orders and injunctions do not generally last for as long as the above orders. They are not intended to resolve the question of your accommodation for good but to tide you over until you can make alternative arrangements or take divorce proceedings so that the court has an opportunity to deal with long-term arrangements for your family property.

If either party wants the terms of the order or the injunction discharged completely you are free to ask the court to make a further order.

Living together whilst the court order is in force

Non-molestation injunctions and personal protection orders do not necessarily mean that you will be living separately, they simply regulate your conduct towards each other. However, an exclusion order will mean that you will be living apart. However, if you both want to give things another try and start living together again, you are perfectly free to do so without referring to the court.

If this is the case and your spouse feels that he/she would rather not have the exclusion order hanging over him then he/she can apply to the court to have it discharged.

Seeing the children when the court order is in force

Provided that your spouse has not been specifically prevented by the court from seeing the children he/she will normally be entitled to do so even though a personal protection order or non molestation order is in force or he/she has been excluded from the home.

However, you may have to be prepared to alter your arrangements over contact to make sure that they do not involve your spouse breaking the court order.

How quickly can you get a court order?

In a normal case, the court will not deal with your application until your spouse has been notified of it and given a chance to attend at court to put his/her side of the story.

If you urgently need help because you or a child of the family are in imminent danger of being seriously injured by your spouse, the court can immediately act without your spouse even knowing that you have made an application. If the court makes an emergency application in this way, the order is described as an "ex parte" order (in the county court). In the magistrate's court it is described as an "expedited order".

As a general rule, you will not be able to obtain an exclusion order by this emergency procedure-the only protection you will be given will be in the form of a non molestation order or personal protection order.

In a really urgent case, it is possible to apply to a judge of the county court for an injunction, even outside court hours, but this is not possible in the magistrate's court, which can only deal with applications during court time.

An emergency order will only be temporary. In the county court, it will last until the earliest possible date when the whole case can be considered in full with an opportunity for your spouse to have his say. An order of the magistrate's court made in an emergency can only last for a maximum of 28 days, even if there has not been an opportunity for a full investigation of the case before then. However, you can apply for it to be renewed at the end of the 28-day period.

The time actually taken to obtain an order, either in an emergency or in the normal way, will depend on all the circumstances-not only what your case involves but also how busy the court is.

Undertakings to the court

If you have made an application to the county court, and your spouse is willing to promise that he/she will not molest you or will move out of the house within a certain length of time he/she may give the court an undertaking that this will be the case. Breach of this undertaking can mean heavy penalties.

Enforcing a court order

If the courts order is not obeyed, then the next step in the process depends very much whether or not there is a "power of arrest" within the court order. This is a special order entitling the police to arrest your spouse straight away if he/she breaks the court order. If the court makes an order prohibiting your spouse from using violence towards you or a child of the family or excluding him/her from the home, and it is satisfied that he/she has already injured you or a child of the family, it can grant a power of arrest. If a power of arrest is granted with your order, and your spouse breaks the courts order by using violence towards you or the child or by entering the house or the surrounding area after he/she has been excluded, you should contact your local police station. The police will normally arrest your spouse at once. If he/she is arrested, he/she will be kept in custody and brought before the court within 24 hours. The court will have to decide what should be done about your spouse's conduct. It can send him/her immediately to prison for whatever period it thinks appropriate. However, this is unlikely to happen if it is the first time he/she has broken the injunction or order, as imprisonment is usually reserved as something of a last resort for people who have persistently disobeyed the courts orders. Alternatively, the court can fine your spouse.

In addition to the above, there are other measures that the court can take. For example, the court may decide to modify the original order in the light of what has happened. If you are not granted a power of arrest, it is up to you, with your solicitor's help, to take steps to bring your spouse back to court if he/she breaks the order so that the court can decide what is to be done. The proceedings described so far in this chapter are "civil proceedings", in other words, they do not involve a criminal prosecution. However, if your spouse assaults you or damages your property, he/she will have committed a criminal offence.

The police would be reluctant to take action though without a power of arrest. If you are dissatisfied that the police are not prosecuting your spouse, you may be able to bring a criminal prosecution against him/her yourself. You should, however, think carefully before going down this road because of the stress and the expense.

9

Other Considerations

Remarriage

You are only free to remarry when your divorce is made final by decree absolute. Before you are allowed to marry in any church or registry office, you will need to produce a copy of the decree absolute.

When you remarry, your entitlement to regular payments from your spouse will cease. This is not the case for children, who will continue to be entitled.

Orders that have already been made in relation to your property and capital will not, however, be affected by your remarriage.

If the spouse who has an obligation to make frequent payments remarries, this will not alter his liability to continue to make these payments. Liability can only be reduced or extinguished if it can be demonstrated that his or her circumstances have changed as a result of re-marriage, which would affect ability to pay.

Once you have remarried, you are no longer entitled to begin a claim for property adjustment orders or for a lump sum payment. This is not the case if you have started the claim before you remarry, you will be allowed to continue with it. You should ensure that all necessary claims to property and other assets are in place before you remarry. Your solicitor will help you with this if necessary. Your rights in relation to children will usually be totally unaffected by remarriage. However, in the unlikely event of your remarrying some one totally unsuitable to be in contact with your children, you could find that your spouse will apply for an order depriving you of contact with them.

Tax and your divorce
Income tax

People generally are affected by three forms of tax during their lives-income tax, inheritance tax and capital gains tax.

Inheritance tax is complicated. This is the tax payable on your assets when you pass away and on any money or property you have transferred within seven years of your death. You will not normally need to involve yourself with inheritance tax at the time of divorce.

Capital gains tax is far more relevant to divorcing couples. This form of taxation is payable on capital gains that are made when you are disposing of property during your lifetime. Her Majesty's Revenue and Customs treat property given away as "disposed of". This therefore attracts a capital gain, or is treated as a capital gain.

Although you will be liable for capital gains tax when you dispose of property, you would not do so if you gave away money. This is exempt. There are also other exemptions from capital gains tax, for example you are permitted to make gains each year on property values. You should check with HMRC for the latest figures.

The tax position when living together as a couple

Income tax. Everyone is entitled to a tax-free element within their income each year, known as the personal allowance. This amount will vary according to your circumstances, i.e. whether you are married or single.

After 6th of April 1990, the system of joining husband and wife's income together for tax purposes ended and a new system introduced. Now husband and wife are taxed separately on their earned and investment income. Each has a single persons allowance.

In addition to this, there is still a married couples allowance which is normally set against a husbands income but can also be set against a woman's earnings. However, both of the partners can claim half of the allowance which will be split equally between them.

Capital gains tax is also no longer combined and a husband and wife will also be taxed independently on his or her capital gains and will be entitled to a tax free allowance to set against them.

While you live together as husband and wife you can dispose of property to each other without incurring a capital gains tax. However, if the property is disposed of later to someone else then a capital gains tax is payable.

The tax position when living apart

Separation will affect your tax position. For tax purposes, you are living apart if you are separated under a court order or a deed of Separation or you are separated in such a way, or circumstance, that your Separation is likely to be permanent.

HMRC imposes special rules during the year that you separate. Each person will have a single persons allowance and there will be a married couple's allowance, which will be split, as it was when you separated. If you have any of the children living with you who are under 16, or over 16 and still undergoing further education at school, university or other college, you may be able to claim an additional personal allowance for the remainder of the year of separation but not if you are already receiving the full married couples allowance. After the end of the tax year in which you separate:

- you both continue to be taxed as individuals on your earned and unearned income. You will each be responsible to HMRC in respect of your own tax.
- normally, you will both only get a single persons allowance

Either one or both of you may be able to claim the additional personal allowance if you are looking after one or more of the children. Separated spouses are treated as single people for the purposes of capital gains tax. During the first year, or the tax year within which you separate you can make tax free disposals to your spouse. After that ends, so does this right.

After divorce
Most of the tax changes experienced by yourself will happen when you cease to live together. The act of divorce only finalizes these changes.

Maintenance payments and income tax
In 1988, the treatment of maintenance payments, and the tax position was simplified. Although certain of the older orders and maintenance agreements remain under older rules, all other orders are subject to the new rules as set out below.

The payer
If the court orders that you make maintenance payments to a spouse, or ex-spouse either for his or her own benefit, or a child's benefit, or you enter into a legally binding agreement to do so then you should get tax relief on the payments.

You will get this tax relief through your PAYE code or tax assessment. Relief for your maintenance payments will continue if you remarry but will cease if your spouse does.

The recipient
The maintenance you receive will be tax-free. This also applies to your children.

Sharing out property and capital gains tax

Until you separate, and in the year of separation, you can make whatever re-allocation of assets between you that you like without any immediate liability to Capital Gains Tax.

After you separate, and following the end of that particular tax year, gains that you make when transferring property to your spouse could be liable to Capital Gains Tax depending on the type of property involved. As stated previously, you can share out savings but if you have to sell an item to pay of your spouse then you may be liable to pay tax.

When you dispose of your house to your spouse, or previous spouse, it is not always possible to escape entirely from Capital Gains Tax. This is because any gain which is made when disposing of a property that was your main home is exempt from Capital Gains Tax provided that you have been absent from it for more than three years and that no other house has replaced it as your residence, or main residence.

Even if you have moved out more than three years ago, you may still escape Capital Gains Tax if you transfer an interest in the house to your spouse as part of a financial settlement on divorce or separation, provided your spouse has continued to occupy the house as her only main home.

Enforcing court orders and agreements

Problems usually arise over payment of maintenance, in that they are sporadic or stop altogether. However, problems do also arise over arrangements for property. Courts can resolve problems such as these.

Maintenance problems

If you have come to a formal agreement with your spouse concerning payment of maintenance and your spouse fails to pay, the courts can order him or her to pay as agreed. This is the same if the order has been made by the court and is broken. The method of enforcement will depend on which court made the order.

Enforcement in the magistrate's court

If the court order has been registered in the magistrate's court, because problems of future payments were foreseen, then it is the responsibility of the magistrate's court to chase up non-payment.

Magistrate's courts can take several different views about non-payment. They can, for example, decide that your spouse should be excused from some or all arrears. This does not excuse your spouse from future liability. The Magistrates court can also make arrangements for your spouse to pay off the arrears in instalments along with the current maintenance due.

An attachment of earnings order can also be made. It is addressed to the employer, if one exists and directs the paying of frequent sums of money from the spouse's earnings. The court can also order that your spouse be sent to prison for non-payment of maintenance. This is usually a last resort but is a frequent occurrence, as Her Majesties Prisons will testify. If you receive regular payments of income support, because of the low level of maintenance paid by your spouse, you may want to make over your maintenance order to the Department of Social Security. This means that the magistrate's court will pay over sums to the DSS instead of you. You will then be entitled to draw full income support, irrespective of what is paid to you by your spouse.

If your order has not been registered in the magistrate's court it will be up to you to take your spouse back before the magistrate's court to get an order to pay. You should keep a clear and accurate record of payments made to you. If your spouse goes abroad, then the act of collecting unpaid maintenance becomes that much harder and you will need help from a solicitor in deciding a way forward.

Child support maintenance

If your case has been referred to the Child Support Agency then the agency will automatically collect the Child Support Maintenance for you if you are in receipt of state benefits and will do so, on request, on other cases. If you receive child support maintenance, the Child Support Agency will automatically review the amount at regular intervals. Either parent has the right to apply to the child support officer for review if the circumstances have changed and the maintenance assessment is likely to be substantially altered as a result.

Variations of agreements in the future

The courts have powers to vary orders at a later date if circumstances change.

Maintenance orders

You are more likely to require a change in the divorce courts maintenance order than in any other court order. Although the court will vary orders, you have to put forward a good case for the change. If you were awarded or ordered to pay a lump sum in one instalment, the court will not be able to alter this order on a subsequent occasion. If the lump sum is paid in more than one instalment then this can be altered. If the court made an order in relation to your property on your divorce neither of you can ask for this order to be varied at a later date. However, if the court granted you "liberty to apply" or ordered a sale on some of your property when it made the order, you can seek further assistance in putting the order into practice.

Changing your will

Like almost everyone, during marriage all of your property and assets (estate) would normally be made out to your partner. However, on breakdown of marriage it is usual for your will, if you have one, to be substantially altered.

If you die without making a will, this is known as dying intestate. If you die intestate before decree absolute of divorce is granted, as a general rule all your personal belongings will pass to your spouse, together with a substantial proportion of your money and your interests in land.

If you die intestate after the divorce is finalized, your spouse will have no automatic right to any of your estate. Your children would probably inherit the estate. However, provided your spouse has not remarried, he or she can make an application to the court for a share of the estate on the grounds that provision for his or her maintenance should have been made after your death.

If you have a will

If you die after decree absolute has been granted leaving a will made before you were divorced, then unless it is clear that your intention is for the former spouses position to be unaffected by the divorce, anything left to him or her will automatically become ineffective, as will any appointment of him as your executor.

If you die before Decree Absolute your spouse will still be able to benefit from the will. It is advisable to produce a fresh will which takes into account your new circumstances following divorce and possible remarriage. Surprisingly, this is one area which is very neglected and which causes a lot of pain and anxiety following divorce and the death of one or other partner.

10

Divorce in Scotland

Scottish Family and Divorce Law is significantly different from that in England and Wales. You can commence divorce proceedings in Scotland if you or your spouse are domiciled in Scotland or if either of you were habitually resident in Scotland for at least a year before starting proceedings.

Grounds for divorce

There is no minimum period you have to wait after marriage before you can bring divorce proceedings. The sole ground for divorce is irretrievable breakdown of marriage: this can be established only by proof of one of the following:

- adultery
- unreasonable behaviour
- desertion for two or more years
- non-cohabitation for two or more years and your spouse consents to the divorce
- non-cohabitation for five or more years.
-

If your spouse has committed adultery you do not have to show that you find it intolerable to live with him or her.

Unreasonable behaviour includes being violent, nagging persistently, abusing the children and being financially irresponsible, as well as negative conduct such as ignoring your spouse or his or her sexual or emotional needs. Non-cohabitation means not living together as any normal married couple would. You can be sharing the same house but be living separate lives. Most divorces are dealt with in the sheriff courts. These are local courts situated in most major towns in Scotland. You can bring proceedings in the area in which you and your spouse have been living for the last forty days. Divorces are also heard in the court of session in Edinburgh. Legal Aid is not available in this court.

There are no decrees nisi or absolute in Scotland. The court grants a single decree of divorce which is immediately effective, although a certain period (14 days in the sheriffs court, 21 days in the court of session) is allowed for appeal.

Getting a divorce

There are two types of procedure: the simplified procedure (usually called a DIY divorce and the ordinary procedure. DIY divorce can only be used where the ground is non-cohabitation for two or five years. In addition, there must be no children of marriage under the age of 16yrs, no financial claims by you or your spouse and no other legal proceedings affecting your marriage waiting to be heard. The divorce must be uncontested and you or your spouse must not be suffering from any mental disorder. As in England, printed forms for d-i-y procedure are available from the court or from a Citizens Advice Bureaux or from the internet. If you cannot get a DIY divorce you will have to use the ordinary procedure. This is more complex and you will almost certainly need a solicitor acting for you.

Separation agreements

Instead of going to court a couple may enter into an agreement specifying aliment for children, which parent they are going to live with, when the other parent can see them or have them to stay (contact)

A Guide to Divorce and the Law

aliment for the wife and what is to happen to the family home for the period from separation to divorce. Separated couples may also enter into agreements as to how their property is to be divided. They can then rely on that agreement and not apply to the divorce court for financial orders.

An agreement cannot prevent later applications to the court relating to the residence of and contact with the children or to the Child Support Agency for maintenance for the children where one of the parents starts receiving certain state benefits.

Ordinary divorce procedure

Proceedings start with your solicitor lodging the initial writ in court. This document sets out briefly the facts of your case and details the orders that you are asking the court to make. A copy of this writ is then served on your spouse. You are called the pursuer and he or she the defender. A copy also has to be served on any person with whom your spouse has committed adultery. The children may be sent a notice telling them about the court proceedings (if a parental rights order is sought) unless the court considers it inappropriate because of the children's age and they will be invited to express their views either in person or in writing. In a divorce action based on either two or five years non-cohabitation, your spouse is also sent a notice warning of the possible financial consequences of divorce (loss of pension rights for example).

In your initial writ you can apply for various interim orders, or you can add them on later. Interim orders last until the divorce is granted, when the position is reviewed and fresh orders granted. Examples of interim orders are:

- interim aliment for you. The CSA deals with maintenance for the children.
- interim residence for and contact with the children.
- an interim interdict (prohibition against violent behaviour or disposal of assets).
- An interdict against taking the children out of Scotland. Your application for this need not be intimated to your spouse so that he or she may get no warning at all.

You can also apply for these remedies separately: they are not available only in divorce proceedings.

Defences
A notice of intention to defend must be lodged within 21 days (42 if the defender is abroad). An options hearing will then be held during which the court will clarify the issues in dispute and decide how to proceed.

Affidavits
An affidavit is accepted by the court as evidence of the facts contained within it. You, your spouse and others can give evidence by affidavit instead of attending court. This is not available unless the action is undefended or uncontroversial.

Reconciliation
You and your spouse can still try to save your marriage even though divorce proceedings have started.

The children
You should show that satisfactory arrangements have been made for any

children under 16. Most couples reach agreement about who is to look after the children. In addition to your own affidavit stating these arrangements the court will require an affidavit from a relative or a person who knows the children well. If the affidavits are satisfactory, the court will accept the arrangements without interviewing the couple.

Joint minute

If you and your spouse can agree on the financial aspects of the divorce and future arrangements for the children before proceedings start, you can ask the court simply to make an appropriate order and your spouse need not defend.

Decree

A decree is a formal document containing the orders made by the court. The financial orders are usually granted at the same time as the divorce, although it is possible for these to be left over for a later hearing if disagreement on this front is holding up the divorce. The court will notify you that a decree has been granted and also notify your spouse if his or her address is known. There is a 14 day period allowed for appeal (21 days in the court of session). After that, an extract (certified copy) of the decree can be obtained from the court which details the orders that the court has made. You will need an extract if you plan to marry again, to prove your divorce or if you want to enforce the orders.

Mediation

There are two kinds of mediation services for family breakdown problems. They can be used at any time before, during or after proceedings. You can either contact the service directly or ask your solicitor to make arrangements. Local mediation services affiliated to Family Mediation Scotland generally help couples resolve disputes relating to the children. Some services may offer mediation on financial issues. Mediation is free but donations are welcome.

Members of Comprehensive Accredited Lawyer Mediators (CALM) deal with the financial aspects of splitting up as well as matters affecting children. The Mediators are all family lawyers accredited as mediators by the Law Society of Scotland. Mediation sessions are usually taken by two lawyers, one male and one female, with a fee charged. Generally two to three sessions of about one and a half hours each are needed. If either of the spouses is legally aided, his or her share of these fees will be paid for.

The home
Before divorce

Most couples own their own homes jointly. If this is the case, both are equally entitled to a share if the home is sold. However, for those couples who do not own jointly, The Matrimonial Homes (Family Protection) (Scotland) Act 1981 gives certain rights if one spouse does not own the home and the other is the sole owner. You are entitled to continue to occupy and live in the home. Consent is required if the home is to be sold. These rights are automatic. Married co-tenants and spouses of sole tenants have similar protection against the tenancy of the home being given up.

Exclusion orders

You can apply to the court for an order excluding your spouse from the family home and immediate vicinity if he or she behaves violently towards you or the children. This order is called an exclusion order and even a sole tenant or owner can be excluded.

Interdicts

Another way of protecting yourself from violence or molestation by your spouse is to apply for a court order (interdict) prohibiting such conduct. Interdicts can be gained quickly, sometimes within a day, depending on the severity of the problem. It is possible also to have a power of arrest added to an interdict. This means that if the order is breached then the police can arrest the offending party.

Orders called non-harassment orders (NHO) might also be available to prevent undesirable conduct. Breach of an NHO is punishable as a criminal offence.

On getting divorced

Orders regarding the home are part of the overall financial settlement. The court on granting divorce may:

- make no order and allow the home to be sold. The proceeds will have been taken into account in any lump sum award made.
- Transfer the ownership (or tenancy) of the home or a share of it, from one spouse to another.
- Regulate who is to occupy the home after divorce.

The children

A decision has to be made concerning the welfare of children. The Children Act 1989 does not apply to Scotland: the legislation applicable is the Children (Scotland) Act 1995. In Scotland, parents have various responsibilities towards their children, such as safeguarding them, advising them and acting on their behalf in legal transactions, and various rights such as deciding where they will live, controlling their upbringing and having contact with them. These responsibilities and rights cease when the child reaches 16.

While the parents live together they share the parental responsibilities and rights. On divorce, the courts may, on application, reallocate these rights. Orders may be unnecessary if the parents are willing to co-operate.

Child abduction

The Scottish provisions of the Child Abduction Act 1984 are different from those of England and Wales. A parent commits a criminal offence by taking a child out of the UK only if:

- the other parent (or someone else) has been awarded custody or has a residence order and has not agreed to the child's removal, or
- the court has interdicted removal.

If your spouse is likely to take the children abroad you should apply for a residence order or interdict at once. You can do so without even applying for divorce.

Financial orders

Many couples will negotiate a financial settlement instead of litigating. Such an agreement is binding and will be set aside only if the court is satisfied that it was not fair and reasonable at the time it was entered into. The court will not look at, still less vet, the agreement unless an application is made to set it aside.

The main financial orders a court can make on divorce are:

- ordering one spouse to pay a lump sum to the other
- Order one spouse to pay the other a periodical allowance-a regular sum each week or month

- Ordering a spouse to pay aliment for the children of the marriage but only if the CSA cannot assess maintenance
- Transfer the ownership of property from one spouse to the other.

The Family Law Act (Scotland) 1985 sets out a series of principles to guide the courts in making financial orders, as follows:

1. Sharing matrimonial assets.

The home and its contents, savings, investments and other assets which you or your spouse own and which were acquired between the date of marriage and the date of separation are matrimonial assets.

2. Balancing economic advantages and disadvantages

The court has to take into account your financial and non-financial contributions to your spouses wealth – and the other way round. Examples include helping with the running costs of the home, sacrificing a career to look after the children or working in your spouses business at an artificially low wage.

3.Sharing Children

Future childcare costs are to be shared. These include any loss of earnings while looking after the children.

4. Financial dependency

Under this principle you are entitled to support for up to three years after divorce to enable you to become self-supporting, if you were financially dependent on your spouse during the marriage.

5. Severe financial hardship

If you are unlikely to be self supporting after divorce you may need support for many years to avoid severe financial hardship.

Aliment for the children

The CSA now assesses maintenance for children up to and including 18 years of age who are still in secondary education. The courts have no power to deal with claims for these children. Certain categories of children are not within the agencies remit and can still be awarded aliment by the courts. The most important of these categories are:

- children aged 19-24 who are undergoing further educational training at a university, college, apprenticeship or so on. Children have to look after themselves once they reach 25 as the parental obligation of aliment ceases then
- a child who has been accepted by you or your spouse as a child of the family. The accepting spouse will have an obligation of aliment. The usual example is a stepfather accepting his wife's children by former marriage.
- Where the parent due to pay aliment is abroad.

The CSA will refuse to assess if the parties have entered into a formal written agreement about aliment, unless one of the parties starts claiming state benefits. The amount of aliment awarded will depend on what the person paying can afford and what the child needs. The previous level of support the child enjoyed is also important.

A child over 11 can apply to the CSA for an assessment of his or her own maintenance. Children over 18 who wish aliment via the courts must claim themselves.

Effect of divorce on your inheritance rights

After divorce, you have no rights to your ex-spouses estate if he or she dies without leaving a will or leaving you nothing. Legacies or other provisions for you in your ex-spouses will are not cancelled by divorce after the date of the will. Generally speaking, you are entitled to take them unless the will makes it clear that you should not.

After divorce, you and your spouse should review any existing will. Changes will probably be highly desirable.

Judicial separation

Instead of divorce you can apply for a judicial separation. The grounds are the same as divorce. The court granting a judicial separation has no power to award a capital sum or order a transfer of property. It can only award aliment for you. The marriage remains so remarriage is not possible. There is limited legal point in opting for judicial separation.

11

Civil Partnerships

A Civil partnership is a legal relationship, which can be registered by two people of the same sex. Same-sex couples, within a civil partnership can obtain legal recognition for their relationship and can obtain the same benefits generally as married couples.

Civil partnerships came into force on 5th December 2005. The first civil partnerships registered in England and Wales took place on 21st December 2005. Civil partners are treated the same as married couples in many areas, including:

- Tax, including inheritance tax
- Employment benefits
- Most state and occupational pension benefits
- Income related benefits, tax credits and child support
- Maintenance for partner and children
- Ability to apply for parental responsibility for a civil partners child
- Inheritance of a tenancy agreement
- Recognition under intestacy rules
- Access to fatal accidents compensation
- Protection from domestic violence
- Recognition for immigration and nationality purposes

The registration of a civil partnership
Two people may register a civil partnership provided they are of the

same sex, not already in a civil partnership or legally married, not closely related and both over 16 although consent of a parent or guardian must be obtained if either of them are under 18.

Registering a civil partnership is a secular procedure and is carried out by the registration service, which is responsible for the registration of births, deaths and marriages. A civil partnership registration is carried out under what is termed a standard procedure, which can be varied to take into account housebound people or people who are ill and are not expected to recover.

The standard procedure for registering a civil partnership

A couple wishing to register a civil partnership just have to decide the date they want to register and where they want the registration to take place. The formal process for registering consists of two main stages-the giving of a notice of intention to register and then the registration of the civil partnership itself.

The first stage, the giving of notice is a legal requirement and both partners have to do this at a register office in the area of a local authority where they live, even if they intend to register elsewhere. The notice contains the names, age, marital or civil partnership status, address, occupation, nationality and intended venue for the civil partnership. It is a criminal offence to give false information. If one of the partners is a non-EAA citizen and subject to immigration controls (see later) there are additional requirements to be fulfilled. Once the notice has been given it is displayed at the relevant register office for 15 days. This provided an opportunity for objections to be made. The civil partnership cannot be registered until after 15 clear days have elapsed from the date of the second person gives notice. Each partner needs to give notice in the area that they have lived for at least seven days. If the couple live in different areas then each will post a notice in their own relevant area. When giving notice they will be asked where they wish the civil partnership to take place.

Residency requirements for a civil partnerships

A couple can register a civil partnership in England and Wales as long as they have both lived in a registration district in England and Wales for at least seven days immediately before giving notice. If one person lives in Scotland and the other lives in England or Wales, the person living in Scotland may give notice there. Officers, sailors or marines on board a Royal Navy ship at sea can give notice to the captain or other commanding officer, providing they are going to register with someone who is resident in England and Wales. Service personnel based outside England and Wales have to fulfil the above residence requirements.

Documentary evidence of name, age and nationality will need to be shown. Passports and birth certificates are the main documents required. Proof of address will be required. If either partner has been married or in a civil partnership before evidence of divorce or dissolution will be required. If either partner is subject to immigration control a document showing entry clearance granted to form a civil partnership will need to be shown, along with a home office certificate of approval and indefinite leave to remain in the UK.

Civil partnership registration

A civil partnership registration can take place in any register office in England and Wales or at any venue that has been approved to hold a civil partnership. Approved premises include stately homes and other prestigious buildings including hotels and restaurants. From 5th December 2005, any venue that has approval for civil marriage is automatically be approved for civil partnerships. A civil partnership cannot be registered at a religious premises. A civil partnership can only be registered between the hours of 8am to 6pm unless one person is seriously ill and is not expected to recover.

A civil partnership is legally registered once the couple have signed the legal document, known as a civil partnership schedule, in the presence of a registrar and two witnesses. On the day, two witnesses will be required. If they wish to do so, the couple will be able to speak to each other the words contained in the schedule:

' I declare that I know of no legal reason why we may not register as each other's civil partner. I understand that on signing this document we will be forming a civil partnership with each other'

No religious service may take place, as the process of forming a civil partnership is entirely secular. A ceremony can be arranged to accompany the actual registration. This ceremony can take place at any venue as long as it is approved.

Costs of registering a civil partnership

The costs here are applicable to 2009/10. Like all other costs they will change from year to year and the current costs should always be ascertained by contacting your local register office.

The current costs are as follows:

- Giving notice of intention to register   £30 (£60 a couple)
- Registration at Register Office   £40

Registration at an approved premises-in this case the cost for attendance by a civil partnership registrar is set by the registration authority in question. A further charge may also be made by the owner for use of the building,

- Cost of civil partnership certificate on the day of registration £8.50 (you should check these costs)
- Further copies of the civil partnership certificate £7

The General Register Office website www.grogo.uk has a search facility if you need to find a local register office or an office any where in the UK.

Changing names

After registering a civil partnership, one partner might want to change their surname to that of their partner. Government departments and agencies will accept civil partnership certificates as evidence for changing surnames. Other private institutions may want a different form of evidence. It is up to the individual to check with the various organisations if they wish to change their surname.

Special circumstances

Variations to the standard procedure can be made in certain circumstances. If a partner is seriously ill and is not expected to recover then a civil partnership can be registered at any time. The 15-day waiting period will not apply. A certificate will need to be provided from a doctor stating that a person is not expected to recover and cannot be moved to a place where civil partnerships take place and that they understand the nature and purpose of signing the Registrar Generals licence.

Housebound people

If one partner is housebound there are special procedures to allow them to register a civil partnership at home. A statement has to be signed, made by a doctor, confirming that this is the case and that the condition is likely to continue for the next three months. The statement must have been made no more than 14 days before notice being given and must be made on a standard form provided by the register office. The normal 15-day period will apply between giving notice and the civil partnership registration.

Detained people

There are special procedures to allow a couple to register a civil partnership at a place where one of them is detained in a hospital or prison. The couple has to provide a statement, made by the prison governor or responsible person confirming that the place where a person is detained can be named in the notice of proposed civil partnership as the place where the registration is to take place. This statement must have been made no more than 21 days prior to notice being given. The normal 15 day waiting period applies.

Gender change

The Gender Recognition Act 2004 enables transsexual people to change their legal gender by obtaining a full Gender Recognition Certificate. Where a transsexual person is married, they cannot obtain a full Gender Recognition Certificate without first ending their existing marriage. However, if they and their former spouse then wish to form a civil partnership with one another without delay, they can do so as soon as the full Gender Recognition Certificate has been issued. In those circumstances, they give notice and register on the same day. More information is available about the process of changing gender on www.grp.gro.uk

Immigration requirements for people subject to immigration controls

The civil partnerships provisions for people subject to immigration control are exactly the same as those in place for marriage. These apply if one partner is a non-EAA (European Immigration Area) citizen and is subject to immigration control, for example in the UK on a visa.

People subject to immigration control who want to give notice of a civil partnership need to do so at a register office designated for this purpose. They are required to produce one of the following as part of that notice:

- Entry clearance granted to form a civil partnership
- A Home Office certificate of approval
- Indefinite leave to remain in the UK.

Registrars are required to report any civil partnerships to the immigration service if they have any suspicions.

Application for leave to remain

Civil partners of British citizens and people settled here can apply for an initial period of two years leave to remain in the UK. If they are still together at the end of that period they can apply for indefinite leave to remain.

Work permit holders and students

Civil partners of people with temporary leave to remain in the UK, such as students and work permit holders, can apply for leave along with their civil partners. A list of Register Offices for people subject to immigration control, can be found at www.ind.homeoffice.gov.uk or phone 0870 606 7766.

Civil partnership registration for two non-EAA citizens

Two non-EAA citizens can register a civil partnership together in the UK as long as they have entry clearance for the purpose of doing so and have resided in the registration district for at least seven days before giving notice. Registering a civil partnership doesn't affect their immigration status.

Registering civil partnerships abroad

If couples wish to register a civil partnership abroad they should contact the Embassy or High Commission in the country concerned. Couples may be asked to obtain a certificate of no impediment.

It may be possible for couples to register at a UK consulate in another country if one of them is a UK national. However, UK consulates will not register civil partnerships if the host country objects or if civil unions or same sex marriage is available in that country.

Armed Forces

Members of the Armed Forces can register civil partnerships overseas in those areas where a Servicing Registering Officer is able to offer this service.

Overseas relationships

It may be the case that a couple has formed a civil union, registered partnership, domestic partnership or same-sex marriage abroad. Couples in those kind of relationships can automatically be recognised in the UK as civil partners without having to register again provided conditions set out in sections 212 to 218 of the Civil Partnership Act are met.

The legislation defines an overseas relationship that can be treated as a civil partnership in the UK as one that is either specified in Schedule

20 to the Civil Partnership Act or one which meets general conditions in the Act and certain other conditions. Schedule 20 of the Act lists countries and relationships that are recognised. Countries listed in the Act are:

- Argentina
- Belgium
- Brazil
- Canada
- Denmark
- Finland
- France
- Germany
- Iceland
- Israel
- Mexico
- Netherlands
- Norway
- Portugal
- South Africa
- Spain
- Sweden
- USA-Vermont-Iowa-Massachusetts-New Hampshire-New York-Vermont-District of Columbia

However, you should check this list, which is current as at 2012 as it changes as countries adopt civil partnerships. A couple who have formed a relationship recognised in one of those countries can be recognised in the UK as civil partners if they are of the same sex, the relationship has been registered with a responsible body in that country, the country were eligible to enter into a civil relationship in that country and all procedural requirements have been fulfilled.

For foreign relationships in countries not listed in Schedule 20 a couple who have formed a relationship can still be recognised as civil partners if the foreign relationship meets the general conditions set out in the Civil Partnerships Act. To find out which foreign relationships are contained within Schedule 20, which is revised periodically, go to www.womenandequalityunit.gov.uk/civilpartnership.htm

Dissolution of relationships formed abroad

Where a couple have formed an overseas relationship and that relationship is treated as a civil partnership in the UK, they may be able to obtain a dissolution, annulment or legal separation here. Legal advice should be sought in this matter.

Family relationships

The law now recognises the role of both civil partners in respect of a child living in their household.

Adoption

Under the Adoption and Children Act 2002, which came into force on 30th December 2005, civil partners may apply jointly to adopt a child.

Parental responsibility

Under the Adoption and Children Act 2002, a person will also be able to acquire parental responsibility for the child of their civil partner. They can do this with the agreement of their civil partner. If the child's other parent also has parental responsibility, both parents must agree. Parental responsibility can also be acquired on application to the court.

Civil partners will have a duty to provide maintenance for each other and any children of the civil partnership.

Social security, tax credits and child support

Entering into a civil partnership will affect entitlements to the benefits and tax credits a person may be receiving. From 5th December 2005, the income of a civil partner has been taken into account when calculating entitlement to income related benefits. These benefits include income support, income based job seekers allowance, pension credit, housing benefit and council tax benefit. For a list of benefits and other advice contact the Benefit Enquiry Line on 0800 882200.

Tax credits

From 5th December 2005 the income of a civil partner has been taken into account when calculating entitlement to child and working tax credits. The Tax Credit Line on 0845 300 3900 can offer further advice.

Child support

From 5th December 2005, civil partners who are parents will be treated in the same way as married partners for Child Support. Also, parents who are living with a same sex partner even where they have not formed a civil partnership will be treated in the same way as parents who live together with an opposite sex partner but who are not married.

For further information contact the Child Support Agency.

Pensions

Survivor benefits in occupational and personal pension schemes. Surviving civil partners will be entitled to a pension based on accrued pension right. New rules for civil partners mean that a surviving partner will benefit from a survivors pension based on the contracted out pension rights accrued by their deceased partner from 1988 to the date of retirement or death if this occurs before retirement. This new rule applies to all contracted out private pension schemes.

State pensions
From 5th December 2005, civil partners have enjoyed most of the same state pension rights as husbands and they will treated the same as husbands and wives after 2010 when the treatment of men and women will be equalised. For more information concerning pensions contact the Pension Service on 0845 6060625.

Tax
From 5th December 2005, civil partners have been treated the same as married couples for tax purposes. Information is available from a local tax office and the HMRC website www.hmrc.gov.uk

Employment rights
Employers are required to treat both married partners and civil partners in the same way. The Employment Equality (Sexual Orientation) Regulations 2003 have been amended to ensure that civil partners receive the same treatment and can bring a claim for sexual orientation discrimination if this is not the case. Other areas where changes are made include flexible working, where a civil partner of a child under six or disabled child under 18 will be able to take advantage of flexible working arrangements. Paternity and adoption leave will now be the right of civil partners More information on paternity and adoption leave and pay can be found on www.dti.gov.uk/workingparents.

Wills

Like all people, couples or not, making a will is the most sensible way of ensuring equitable disposal of your assets in accordance with your wishes. The most valuable asset is usually a home and this will automatically vest in a civil partner after death of the other partner, whether or not a will expressly states this. All other property belonging to one of the civil partners will be disposed of according to the will. If a person has a will and then registers a civil partnership it will be revoked automatically unless it expressly states otherwise. If a person dies without making a will there are special legal rules which determine how the estate of the deceased should be shared amongst that persons relatives. Under the new law, if a civil partner dies intestate then his or her civil partner can receive a maximum of £200,000 from the estate and a half share of the amount that is left. If the deceased had children then the amount which the surviving civil partner automatically receives is £125,000 and a half share of the rest. You should however check these figures from time to time.

An application to the court can be made if a surviving civil partner feels that the will doesn't make adequate provision for them.

Life assurance

Civil partners can hold life insurance on their partner's life on the same basis as a married person. In the event of an accident caused by negligence of another then the civil partner can claim compensation and can claim bereavement damages, currently £10,000. Similarly, someone living with the deceased as though they had been in a civil partnership for two years prior to date of death will also be entitled to claim compensation as a dependant.

Tenancy rights

The general effect of the Civil Partnerships Act has been to give the same rights to civil partners as married couples. The Act also equalises the rights of same sex couples who are living together as if they were civil partners and their families with those of unmarried opposite sex couples.

Dissolution of a civil partnership

A civil partnership ends only on the death of one of the civil partners, or on the dissolution of the partnership or a nullity order or a presumption of death order by the court.

The usual route is for one of the partners to seek a dissolution order to terminate the civil partnership. Other options are available. If one party, for example, did not validly consent as a result of duress, mistake or unsoundness of mind, then a nullity order may be sought from the court. Or if both civil partners do not wish to terminate the partnership one of them may ask the court for a separation order.

The dissolution process

Whoever decides to end the civil partnership may need to seek legal advice. The case will usually be dealt with by a civil partnership proceedings county court, although complex cases will be referred to the high court. There are currently ten courts able to deal with civil partnership proceedings. These are listed below:

Birmingham
Brighton
Bristol
Cardiff
Chester
Exeter

Leeds
Manchester
Newcastle
Principal Registry of the family Division

There are a number of leaflets issued by the courts which describe the dissolution process in detail. These are listed under useful information at the back of this book.

To end a civil partnership the applicant (petitioner) must prove to the court that the civil partnership has irretrievably broken down. Proof of an irretrievable breakdown is based on the following:

- Unreasonable behaviour by both other civil partner
- Separation for two years with the consent of the other civil partner
- Separation for five years without the consent of the other civil partner
- If the other civil partner has deserted the applicant for a period of two years or more.

Nullity

In exceptional circumstances one party to a civil partnership may decide to seek a court order (a 'Nullity' order) to annul the civil partnership.

Separation

The grounds on which a separation order may be sought are exactly the same as those for a dissolution order. The end result is different, as a person whose civil partnership has been dissolved is free to marry or form a new partnership whereas a person who has separated remains a civil partner.

Property and financial arrangements

If a civil partnership is ending or if the couple are separating, they will need to decide what happens to any property belonging to them. If they agree on a division they can ask the court to approve the agreement. If they cannot agree they can ask the court to decide. The court has power to make a range of orders In relation to property and other assets including income:

- The court can make an order that one civil partner pay maintenance to the other either for the benefit of the civil partner or for the benefit of any children of the relationship. These orders are known as financial provision orders.
- The court can make an order which will adjust the property rights of the civil partners as regards to property and other assets which they own, either together or separately. This may, for example, mean ordering the transfer and ownership of property from one civil partner to another for that persons benefit or the benefit of any children (known as property adjustment orders)
- The court can make an order in relation to the future pension entitlement of one of the civil partners in favour of the other. This order can relate to occupational pensions, personal pensions and other annuities (known as pension sharing orders)

Financial provision orders for maintenance can be made before a civil partnership has been ended or as separation order granted by the court. Property adjustment and pension sharing orders only take legal effect once dissolution, separation or nullity order has been made by the court.

Even if the couple have been able to agree on maintenance and other property issues they should seek professional advice on such issues. In most cases the solicitor dealing with the end of the civil partnership will be able to provide appropriate advice.

If you require details of local solicitors with experience in this are you should go to www.clsdirect.org.uk/index.isp or phone the community legal service on 0845 3454345.

Care of children

Agreeing arrangements for the care of any children should be the first priority of couples who are ending their civil partnerships or choosing to live apart through separation.

If a couple decide to end the civil partnership the court will want to ensure that both partners are happy with the arrangements for looking after children. If a couple are unable to agree the court will decide for them, or may do so, as part of the dissolution proceedings.

USEFUL INFORMATION

This book is designed to give you as much information as possible and to prepare you for the legalities of the divorce procedure. There are many other sources of information about divorce and the various aspects of divorce such as welfare benefits etc. The following are some of the more useful addresses and web sites.

Alcoholics Anonymous
National Helpline 0845 769 7555
Web site: www.alcoholicsanonymous.org.uk

Asian Family Counselling Service
Suite 51
Windmill Place
2-4 Windmill Lane
Southhall
Middlesex
UB2 4NJ
Tel: 0208 571 3933

Association for Shared Parenting
0121 449 1716
Web site:
www.sharedparenting.org.uk

Both Parents Forever
39 Cloonmore Avenue
Orpington
Kent BR6 9LE
Tel: 01689 854343

Child Abduction Unit
Official Solicitors department
4th Floor
81 Chancery Lane
London WC2 1DD
Tel: 020 7911 7045/7047

Child Poverty Action Group
94 White lion Street
London N1 9PF
Tel: 020 7837 7979
Fax: 020 7837 6414
Web site: www.cpag.org.uk

Child Support Agency
Enquiry line tel: 08457 133133
Web site: www.dss.org.uk

Divorce Registry
First Avenue House
42-49 High Holborn
London WC1V 6NP
Tel: 020 7947 6000

Family Law Consortium
2 Henrietta Street
London WC2E 8PS
Tel: 020 7420 5000
Email:flc@tflc.co.uk
Web site: www.tflc.co.uk

Gingerbread
Single Parent Helpline 0808 802 0925
Web site: www.gingerbread.org.uk.

A support organisation for lone parents and their families, with around
20 centres in the country.

Women's Aid
PO Box 391
Bristol BS9 7WS
National helpline: Tel: 0800 2000247

National Council for the Divorced and Separated
National Secretary
68 Parkes Hall Road
Woodsetton
Dudley
DY1 3SR
07041 478120
Web site: www.ncds.org.uk

National Family Mediation
Margaret Jackson Centre
4 Barnfield Hill
Exeter
Devon EX1 1SR
10392271610

Relate National Marriage Guidance Council
National Phoneline 0300 100 1234

Website: www.relate.org.uk

Scottish Marriage Care
72 Waterloo Street
Glasgow
G2 7DA
0845 271 2711
www.ScottishMarriageCare.org

Scottish Legal Aid Board
44 Drumsheugh Gardens
Edinburgh EH3 7SW
0131 226 7061

Scottish Women's Aid
132 Rose Street
Edinburgh EH2 3JD
0131 226 6606

Further information-civil partnerships

Stonewall can provide information on www.stonewall.org.uk Tel
0800050 20 20

Northern Ireland information on civil partnerships go to
www.groni.gov.uk/index/civil partnerships

For information on civil partnership in Scotland go to
www.scotlandcivilpartnerships.co.uk

Tax-contact your local tax office or go to www.hmrc.gov.uk

Pensions-contact the pension service on 0845 6060265

Social security benefits-contact the benefit enquiry line on 0800 882200

Tax credits contact the tax Credits help line on 0845 3003900

Child Benefit- contact the child Benefit Help line on 08453021444 or e-mail child.benefit@hmrc.gsi.gov.uk
Child Support agency- contact 08457 133133

Immigration-contact the immigration and Nationality Bureau on 0870 667766 or go to www.ind.homeoffice.gov.uk

Relationship support – contact relate on 0845 4561310

Domestic Violence – 0800 2000247 24 hour freephone

Broken Rainbow-LGTB domestic violence forum on 0845 2604460.

LIST OF THE MAIN COUNTY COURT FORMS AND APPLICATIONS USED IN DIVORCE/DISSOLUTION PROCEEDINGS. THE MAIN FORMS FOR BOTH DIVORCE AND DISSOLUTION HAVE BEEN AMALGAMATED.

Leaflets to read before commencing divorce:/dissolution

D183 ABOUT DIVORCE/DISSOLUTION
D184 I WANT A DIVORCE/DISSOLUTION-WHAT DO I DO?
D185 CHILDREN AND DIVORCE
D186 THE RESPONDENT HAS REPLIED TO MY PETITION-WHAT DO I DO?
D187 I HAVE A DECREE NISI-WHAT DO I DO NEXT?
D190-I WANT TO APPLY FOR A FINANCIAL ORDER

The forms (which can be obtained from www.hmcourtservice.org

1. PETITION FOR DIVORCE/Dissolution of Civil Partnership (form D8)
2. Notes for guidance (Petition)
3. Statement of Arrangements for Children (form D8A)
4. Notice of Application (form D11)
5. Affidavit in support of an application to dispense with service of the petition on the respondent (form D13b)
6. Notice of Application for Decree Nisi to be made Absolute (form D36)
7. Affidavit of means (form D75)

Appendix I

Form D8 Divorce/dissolution of civil partnership Petition

Notes to Divorce Petition

Divorce/dissolution/ (judicial) separation petition

To be completed by the Court	
Name of court	
Case No.	
Date received by the court	
Date issued	
Time issued	

Notes to Petitioners

- This form should be used if you are making an application to the court for divorce/dissolution to end your marriage or civil partnership or (judicial) separation from your spouse or civil partner.

- Before completing this form, please read the supporting notes for guidance on completing the form.

- Please answer all questions. If you are unsure of the answer to any question, or you do not think that it applies to you, please indicate this on the form.

- If there is not enough room on the form, you may continue on a separate sheet. Please put your name, the Respondent's (your spouse/civil partner) name, and the number of the Part the information relates to, at the top of your continuation sheet.

- If completing this form by hand, please use **black ink and BLOCK CAPITAL LETTERS** and tick the boxes that apply.

See the supporting notes for guidance

I, _____ (please state your full name)

apply for a ☐ divorce

☐ dissolution

☐ (judicial) separation

in respect of my ☐ marriage

☐ civil partnership

and give the following details in support of my application.

continued over the page ⇨

Part 1 About you (the Petitioner) and the Respondent (your spouse/civil partner)

See the supporting notes for guidance

Petitioner

My current name is
First name(s) (in full)

Last name

My address is (including postcode)

Postcode

My date of birth is
D D / M M / Y Y Y Y

My occupation is

I am
☐ male   ☐ female

Respondent

The Respondent's current name is
First name(s) (in full)

Last name

The Respondent's address is (including postcode)

Postcode

The Respondent's date of birth is
D D / M M / Y Y Y Y

The Respondent's occupation is

The Respondent is
☐ male   ☐ female

Part 2 Details of marriage or civil partnership

See the supporting notes for guidance

On the   day of   [19   ] [20   ]

(insert your name exactly as it appears on your marriage/civil partnership certificate)

☐ married   ☐ formed a civil partnership with

(insert the name of the Respondent exactly as it appears on your marriage/civil partnership certificate)

at

(insert the place where the marriage/civil partnership was formed, exactly as it appears on your marriage/civil partnership certificate)

A certified copy of your marriage/civil partnership certificate must be sent to the court with this completed petition (see supporting notes for guidance).

Part 3 Jurisdiction

See the supporting notes for guidance

The Respondent and I last lived together as ☐ husband and wife ☐ civil partners
at

Address

The court has jurisdiction to hear this case under

☐ Article 3(1) of the Council Regulation (EC) No 2201/2003 of 27 November 2003

or

☐ the Civil Partnership (Jurisdiction and Recognition of Judgments) Regulations 2005

on the following grounds

☐ The Petitioner and Respondent are both habitually resident in England and Wales

☐ Other (please state any other connection(s) on which you wish to rely)

or

☐ The court has jurisdiction other than under the Council Regulation on the basis that no court of a Contracting State has jurisdiction under the Council Regulation and the ☐ Petitioner ☐ Respondent is domiciled in England and Wales on the date when this application is issued

or

☐ The court has jurisdiction other than under the Civil Partnership (Jurisdiction and Recognition of Judgments) Regulations on the basis that no court has, or is recognised as having jurisdiction as set out in the Regulations, and

either:

☐ the ☐ Petitioner ☐ and/or the Respondent is domiciled in England or Wales

or

☐ the Petitioner and Respondent registered as civil partners of each other in England or Wales and it would be in the interests of justice for the court to assume jurisdiction in this case.

continued over the page ➪

Part 4 Other proceedings or arrangements

See the supporting notes for guidance

☐ There are and/or have been

☐ proceedings in any court in England and Wales or elsewhere with reference to the

☐ marriage
☐ civil partnership
☐ or to any child of the family
☐ or between the Petitioner and Respondent with reference to any property of either or both of them

(please enter details below)

```

```

or

☐ no other proceedings in any court in England and Wales or elsewhere.

☐ This is an application based on five years' separation and

☐ agreement has been made or is proposed to be made between the parties for the support of the Petitioner (and any child of the family)

(please enter details below)

```

```

or

☐ no agreement has been made or is proposed to be made.

Part 5 The fact(s)

See the supporting notes for guidance

I apply for a

☐ divorce on the ground that the marriage has broken down irretrievably, or
☐ dissolution on the ground that the civil partnership has broken down irretrievably, or
☐ (judicial) separation

and

I rely on the following fact(s) in support of my application:

☐ The Respondent has committed adultery and the Petitioner finds it intolerable to live with the Respondent (this fact is not applicable in relation to a civil partnership)

☐ The Respondent has behaved in such a way that the Petitioner cannot reasonably be expected to live with the Respondent

☐ The Respondent has deserted the Petitioner for a continuous period of at least two years immediately preceding the presentation of this petition

☐ The parties to the marriage/civil partnership have lived apart for a continuous period of at least two years immediately preceding the presentation of the petition and the Respondent consents to a decree/order being granted

☐ The parties to the marriage/civil partnership have lived apart for a continuous period of at least five years immediately preceding the presentation of the petition.

Part 6 Statement of case

See the supporting notes for guidance

(in all cases, please state briefly any relevant details about the fact(s) on which you rely)

Part 7 Details of the children

See the supporting notes for guidance

Children of the family

Full names of the children of the family	Gender		Date of birth (or state if over 18)	Over 16 but under 18 and in education, training or working full time	(a) Child of both parties	(b) Other child of the family
	male	female				
	☐	☐	D D / M M / Y Y Y Y	☐	☐	☐
	☐	☐	D D / M M / Y Y Y Y	☐	☐	☐
	☐	☐	D D / M M / Y Y Y Y	☐	☐	☐
	☐	☐	D D / M M / Y Y Y Y	☐	☐	☐
	☐	☐	D D / M M / Y Y Y Y	☐	☐	☐
	☐	☐	D D / M M / Y Y Y Y	☐	☐	☐

Statement of arrangements for children
See the supporting notes for guidance

☐ I attach a completed statement of arrangements in respect of those children of the family who are either aged under 16, or aged under 18 and at school, college, or in training for a trade, profession or vocation

or

☐ No statement of arrangements is attached, because there are no children of the family, or no children of the family are either aged under 16 or aged under 18 and at school, college, or in training for a trade, profession or vocation.

5

Children of either party who are not children of the family

Full names of the children of either party who are not children of the family	Gender		Date of birth (or state if over 18)	Born to or adopted by Petitioner	Born to or adopted by Respondent
	male	female	D D / M M / Y Y Y Y		
			D D / M M / Y Y Y Y		
			D D / M M / Y Y Y Y		
			D D / M M / Y Y Y Y		
			D D / M M / Y Y Y Y		
			D D / M M / Y Y Y Y		

Part 8   Special assistance or facilities if you attend court

See the supporting notes for guidance

If you are required to attend court during these proceedings will you need any special assistance or facilities?

☐ Yes (please supply details below)   ☐ No

continued over the page ⇨

Part 9 Service details

See the supporting notes for guidance

☐ I am not represented by a solicitor in these proceedings

☐ I am not represented by a solicitor in these proceedings but am receiving advice from a solicitor

☐ I am represented by a solicitor in these proceedings and all documents for my attention should be sent to my solicitor whose details are as follows:

Box 1 Solicitor's details

Name of solicitor	
Name of firm	

Address to which all documents should be sent for service	Telephone no.	
	Fax no.	
	DX no.	
Postcode ☐☐☐☐ ☐☐☐	Your ref.	

E-mail	

Box 2 Petitioner's address for service

Address (including postcode)

Postcode ☐☐☐☐ ☐☐☐

Box 3 Respondent's address for service

Address (including postcode)

Postcode ☐☐☐☐ ☐☐☐

Box 4 Co-Respondent's details, if any

☐ There is no Co-Respondent

☐ There is a Co-Respondent whose details are as follows:

First Name	
Last Name	

Address (including postcode)

Postcode ☐☐☐☐ ☐☐☐

Part 10

Prayer

The Petitioner therefore prays

(1) The application

☐ That the ☐ marriage ☐ civil partnership be dissolved

or

☐ That the Petitioner be (judicially) separated from the Respondent.

(2) Costs (if you wish to claim costs from the Respondent or Co-Respondent)

☐ That the ☐ Respondent ☐ Co-Respondent shall be ordered to pay the costs of this application

(3) Financial Order (if you wish to make an application for a Financial Order)

☐ (a) That the Petitioner may be granted the following Financial Order(s):

☐ an order for maintenance pending suit

☐ periodical payments order

☐ secured provision order

☐ lump sum order

☐ property adjustment order

☐ order under section 24B, 25B or 25C of the Act of 1973 (Pension Sharing/Attachment Order)

☐ (b) **For the children**

☐ a periodical payments order

☐ a secured provision order

☐ a lump sum order

☐ a property adjustment order

Signed [   ]   Dated [D | D | / | M | M | / | Y | Y | Y | Y]

Supporting notes for guidance on completing a divorce/dissolution/(judicial) separation petition

Important

You should complete this petition if you wish to make an application to the court to dissolve a marriage or civil partnership or if you wish to obtain a (judicial) separation from your spouse or civil partner. You can only apply for a divorce/dissolution if you have been in your marriage or civil partnership for at least one year.

In this form any reference to a marriage certificate or civil partnership certificate means a certified copy of the entry in the Register of Marriages or Register of Civil Partnerships. If you do not have the original marriage/civil partnership certificate, you can apply for a certified copy from the General Register Office or from the relevant Register Officer. Please see leaflet **D183 – About Divorce/ Dissolution** or **D192 – About (Judicial) Separation** for more details, copies of which can be obtained from either a family county court or by going to www.justice.gov.uk.

If you entered into a religious marriage as well as a civil marriage, these divorce proceedings may not dissolve the religious part of your marriage. It is important that you contact the relevant religious authority which authorised the marriage to see whether or not you should take steps to dissolve that marriage. If you do not dissolve the religious marriage, this could have consequences for you and your children.

In cases of urgent applications it may be possible for you to provide an undertaking to the court to deliver the original or a certified copy of the marriage/civil partnership certificate to the court at a later date.

If you are attaching any order of the High Court or a county court to your petition, it must be a sealed copy of the order (that is, a copy that has been stamped with the seal of the court). If you are attaching an order made by a Family Proceedings Court/magistrates' court, it must be a certified copy (a copy certified by a court officer to be a true copy of the original order), or a copy that has been stamped with the seal of the originating court. If you are in any doubt about what is needed, please contact the court where you are applying for assistance.

Take or send the completed application form to the court together with the court fee and any documents you are attaching in support of your application. You will also need to give the court a copy of the petition and documents for each Respondent. If you are not sure about the court fee payable for your petition, or you think that you may be exempt from paying all or part of the fee, you can go to www.justice.gov.uk or contact the court for more information.

Complete the form as fully as you are able. If the form is not fully completed the court may be unable to issue your petition and this may delay your case.

Assistance in completing the form

The notes below will help you to complete the form. However if you are unsure about any of the questions or how to answer them you may wish to seek legal advice.

Page 1: Insert the full name by which you are currently known, and then confirm what you are applying for by ticking the appropriate box.

Part 1: About you (the Petitioner) and the Respondent

You are known as the Petitioner. Your spouse or civil partner is known as the Respondent. You should enter your current details and the Respondent's current details as fully as you know them, making sure you enter the names by which you are both currently known.

If you do not wish to disclose your or your child(ren)'s address, for example because you may feel threatened by the Respondent knowing where you live, or because there is a history of domestic violence, you can leave the details blank and complete Confidential contact details, form **C8**.

Occupation
Please give your occupation and that of the Respondent. If you are not in current employment, please state 'Unemployed/retired/carer' or some other description of your situation.

Part 2: Details of marriage/civil partnership

It is important that the details are entered **exactly** as they are shown on your marriage or civil partnership certificate.

You should attach a certified copy of the marriage/civil partnership certificate together with any other supporting documents regarding any change of name (such as a certified copy of a change of name deed). Photocopies cannot be accepted. If you married or entered into a civil partnership in a foreign country and your marriage/civil partnership certificate is in the language of that country, you must provide a translation of the certificate into English, or Welsh in a court in Wales, from an authorised person (a person authorised for translations). The translation should be signed by a notary public or be authenticated by a statement of truth.

When giving the place at which the marriage/civil partnership was formed you should write the exact words contained in the marriage/civil partnership certificate, including both the printed and written words, which come after the phrase 'Marriage solemnised at' or 'Civil Partnership formed at'.

For example:

- For a marriage in a Register Office: 'The Register Office, in the District of ....
  in the County of ....'

- For a marriage which took place in a church: '.. Church,
  in the Parish of .... in the County of ....'

- For a civil partnership: '.................... in the Registration Authority of ....'

Part 3: Jurisdiction

It is important to be sure that the court has jurisdiction (is able as a matter of law) to deal with your application. Jurisdiction depends on you and/or the Respondent having a specific connection to England and Wales, which may be a connection listed in one of the Regulations referred to below, or a connection which gives rise to the court's 'residual jurisdiction'. It is possible for you to have a connection under more than one option.

Jurisdiction under the Council Regulation or Civil Partnership Regulations
The principal connections that give the court jurisdiction are set out in the following provisions:

- for matrimonial proceedings, Article 3(1) of Council Regulation (EC) No 2201/2003 of 27 November 2003; and

- for civil partnership proceedings, the Civil Partnership (Jurisdiction and Recognition of Judgments) Regulations 2005.

If you consider that the court has jurisdiction to hear the case under one of these provisions you should
- tick the appropriate box to show which of these provisions applies; and
- then state the connection(s) ('the grounds') on which you rely to show that the court has jurisdiction.

The relevant connections are set out below. These connections depend on where you or the Respondent have your 'habitual residence' or your 'domicile'.

Habitual Residence – This is the country where you live voluntarily and for settled purposes (such as work, training, family life), apart from temporary or occasional absences. You must spend a substantial amount of time in a place to be habitually resident there.

Domicile – This is the country which you consider to be your permanent home.

Note: If your spouse/civil partner lives in or is a national of another country, they may have the option of issuing proceedings abroad, and this could prevent your case from continuing here.

The relevant connections
The court will have jurisdiction to hear your case under the Council Regulation or the Civil Partnership Regulations if any of the following connections applies on the date on which your petition is issued. You should state which of the connections matches your situation. You do not need to specify more than one, but if more than one connection applies, you may state more if you wish. **If your spouse/civil partner is not, or may not be, habitually resident in England and Wales, you should state all the connections that apply.**

The connections are that:

- The Petitioner and the Respondent are habitually resident in England and Wales.
- The Petitioner and Respondent were last habitually resident in England and Wales and the [Petitioner*] [or] [the Respondent*] still reside there (*specify as appropriate).
- The Respondent is habitually resident in England and Wales.
- The Petitioner is habitually resident in England and Wales and has resided there for at least a year immediately prior to the presentation of the petition.
- The Petitioner is domiciled and habitually resident in England and Wales and has resided there for at least six months immediately prior to the petition.
- (in a matrimonial case only) The Petitioner and Respondent are both domiciled in England and Wales.

If you and the Respondent are both habitually resident in England and Wales, you should tick the box next to that statement.

If this does not apply to you, or if you wish to rely on any additional or alternative connection(s), please tick 'other' and write in the box any of the other connections on which you rely.

Residual jurisdiction
If none of the above applies, the court may still have jurisdiction on an alternative basis (known as the residual jurisdiction) outside the Regulations. The connection which will give such residual jurisdiction will depend on whether the proceedings are matrimonial or civil partnership proceedings.

For matrimonial proceedings, the court has jurisdiction on a residual basis if:

- no court in any Contracting State (that is, no court in an EU Member State) has jurisdiction under the Council Regulation (because neither the Petitioner nor Respondent is habitually resident in any other Contracting State, nor is there any Contracting State of which they are both nationals, or in the case of the UK and Ireland, in which they are both domiciled); and

- either the Petitioner or the Respondent is domiciled in England and Wales on the date when the petition is issued.

If this option matches your situation you should tick the box next to the appropriate statement and state whether the Petitioner or the Respondent is domiciled in England and Wales.

For civil partnership proceedings, the court has jurisdiction on a residual basis if no court has, or is recognised as having, jurisdiction under the Civil Partnership (Jurisdiction and Recognition of Judgments) Regulations, and either:

- the Petitioner or the Respondent is domiciled in England or Wales

or

- the Petitioner and the Respondent registered as civil partners of each other in England and Wales and it would be in the interests of justice for the court to assume jurisdiction in this case.

If either option matches your situation, you should:

- tick the box next to the appropriate statement; and

- then tick the box by the connection which matches.

If none of the connections described above, whether under the Regulations or residual jurisdiction, matches your situation, the court will not have jurisdiction to deal with your application.

If you are completing this form and need help in deciding which connection applies, you should seek legal advice particularly in international cases.

Part 4: Other proceedings or arrangements

You should indicate, if there have been other proceedings in England and Wales, or elsewhere, concerning:

- your marriage/civil partnership

- any child of the family

- any property belonging to either you or to the Respondent.

This includes any proceedings relating to the marriage/civil partnership, or to any child of the family even if the proceedings have now finished or were abandoned without a final decision being made.

You should give details of the name of the court in which the proceedings took place, details of the order(s) which were made, details of any future hearings and, if proceedings were about your marriage/ civil partnership, say whether you and the Respondent resumed living together as husband and wife/civil partners after the order was made.

If there have been proceedings in a court outside England and Wales which have affected the marriage/ civil partnership, or may affect it, please give the name of the country and the court in which they are taking/have taken place, the date the proceedings were begun and the names of the parties, details of the order(s) made and if no order has yet been made, the date of any future hearing(s).

If your application is based on five years' separation you should answer the second question as appropriate and enter full details of any arrangements made.

Part 5: The fact(s)

Tick the appropriate box to indicate whether you are applying for a divorce (in the case of a marriage) or a dissolution (in the case of a civil partnership), or for a (judicial) separation in respect of your marriage/ civil partnership. Delete the words that do not apply within the statements.

If you are applying for a divorce/dissolution, at least one year must have passed since you married/ entered into a civil partnership before you issue the application.

If you are relying on the facts of two years' desertion, two years' separation with consent or five years' separation, the relevant time period must have passed before you issue the application at the court. E.g. separation or desertion was on 1 March 2010, the first day that an application can be issued is 2 March 2012 (or 2015 in the case of 5 years separation).

Tick the appropriate box(es) to indicate the fact(s) you intend to rely on to prove your application.

Part 6: Statement of case

This space is provided for you to give details of the allegations, which you are using to prove the facts given in Part 5. In most cases one or two sentences will do.

In the case of marriage only, if you have alleged adultery give:

• the date(s) and place(s) where the adultery took place.

You do not have to name the person with whom your spouse is alleged to have committed adultery unless the allegation is likely to be disputed.

If you have alleged unreasonable behaviour give:

• details of a course of conduct, or, particular incidents, including dates, but it should not be necessary to give more than about half a dozen examples of the more serious incidents, including the most recent.

If you have alleged desertion give:

• the date of desertion
• brief details of the circumstances of the desertion
• confirmation that you have lived separately since the date of desertion.

If you have alleged either two or five years' separation give:

• the date of separation
• brief details of how the separation came about
• (in the case of two years' separation) confirmation that the Respondent consents to a decree/order being granted.

In all cases, please give any other relevant details about the fact(s) on which you rely.

If you need more space, you may continue on a separate sheet. You must put your name, the Respondent's name and Part 6 Statement of Case at the top of the continuation sheet.

Part 7: Details of the children

This part asks for details of children of the family. 'Children of the family' includes:

(a) Children born to both you and the Respondent or adopted by both of you;

(b) Other children treated by both of you as children of the family: for example your own or the Respondent's children, or children adopted by one of you;

Any children in these categories should be included on your petition.

For each child you should state:

- their full names, including surname
- their gender
- their date of birth, or you must if applicable state that they are over 18
- if the child is over 16 but under 18 you must state whether he or she is at school or college, or training for a trade, profession or vocation, or is working full time
- whether they fall under (a) or (b) above.

Statement of arrangements for children
If you or the Respondent have any children of the family:

- under 16
- over 16 but under 18 if they are at school or college, university or are training for a trade, profession or vocation

you **must** complete the statement of arrangements for children form. This form is available from the court and online at www.justice.gov.uk.

Before you send your divorce/dissolution/(judicial) separation petition to the court you should try to reach an agreement with your spouse/civil partner about the proposals for the children's future. There is space for your spouse/civil partner to sign at the end of the statement of arrangements for children form if agreement is reached. If your spouse/civil partner does not agree with the proposals they will have the opportunity at a later stage to state why and make their own proposals.

The completed statement of arrangements for children must be signed by you and, if it is agreed, by the Respondent as well. You will need to submit a copy of the completed form whether or not the Respondent has signed it, when you send your divorce/dissolution/(judicial) separation petition to the court together with a copy for the Respondent. If you are attaching health reports please supply one additional copy of the reports (2 copies in total).

You should enter details of all children who are not children of the family e.g. any children who have been born to or adopted by either you or the Respondent, in the table provided.

If there are no children of the family, or no children under the ages specified please tick the second box.

Part 8: Special assistance or facilities if you attend Court

If you or the Respondent need special assistance and/or special facilities due to a disability or impairment, please set out your requirements in full. The court staff will need to know, for example, if you want documents to be supplied in an alternative format, such as Braille or large print. They will also need to know about any specific requirements you may have on the day of the hearing, such as wheelchair access, a hearing loop, or a sign language interpreter. If you require a foreign language interpreter and are unable to provide your own, you may request that one is booked by the court.

The court staff will get in touch with you about your requirements. It is important that you make the court aware of all your needs. If you do not, any hearing may have to be delayed or adjourned to another date.

Part 9: Service details

Throughout the divorce/dissolution/(judicial) separation process, the court will be required to send documents to either one or all of the parties in the case, depending on the stage which the proceedings have reached. This is known as service of the documents.

Please complete the boxes in this section as follows:

Box 1 – If you have a solicitor acting for you, you must insert their details here.

Box 2 – This is the address to which the court will send all documentation for the Petitioner. If you have solicitors acting for you then enter 'as above'.

Please note that if you indicate that you have a solicitor acting for you the Court will only correspond with them. Any questions that you may have about your case should be directed to your solicitor.

Box 3 – This is the address to which the court will send all documentation for the Respondent. If the Respondent does not live in England and Wales, they may be given extra time to file documents. Please check with the court for more details.

Box 4 – Any additional people in the case, for example if you name another person in a case of adultery or an improper association with another person, that person will be known as a Co-Respondent and their address for service of all court documents should be entered here. You do not have to name the person with whom your spouse is alleged to have committed adultery unless the allegation is likely to be disputed. In addition, unless you have permission from the court, you should not name a Co-Respondent if they are under the age of 16 or are the alleged victim of rape committed by the Respondent (see Paragraph 2.1 of Practice Direction 7A).

Part 10: Prayer

The prayer of the petition is your request to the court. You should consider carefully the claims which you wish to make. You should adapt the prayer to suit your claims.

(1) The application

Confirm what you are applying for.

(2) Costs

If you wish to claim that the Respondent or Co-Respondent pay your costs you must do so in your petition. It is not possible to make a claim after a decree/order has been granted. The court will not normally make a costs order where the application is based on 5 years separation.

(3) Financial Order

If you need the court to resolve any dispute over finances you can apply for a financial order. This can deal with property, maintenance, a lump sum payment and/or pensions. An application for a financial order for yourself can only be made before you remarry or enter into a new civil partnership. For more details please see leaflet **D190 – I want to apply for a financial order**.

If you do not complete this section now, but later decide to apply for a financial order, you may be at a financial disadvantage.

If you wish to apply for any of these orders, you should indicate which orders you seek.

You are advised to consult a solicitor if you are unsure about completing this section or about which order(s) you require.

If you complete this section or you later decide to apply for a financial order, you will need to complete and file a Form A to proceed with your application when you are ready to do so.

You can apply to the court for a financial order for any child(ren) of the family in connection with the divorce/dissolution/(judicial) separation proceedings, but the court may only make a periodical payments order for a child if:

- you and the respondent have made a written agreement about child maintenance;
- the child is a stepchild of the Respondent;
- the child or the person with care of the child or the absent parent of the child is **not** habitually resident in the United Kingdom;
- payments are sought in addition to child support maintenance paid under a Child Support Agency calculation;
- the payments are to meet expenses arising from a child's disability;
- the payments are to meet expenses incurred by a child in being educated or training for work;
- the Child Support Agency does not have power to make a maintenance calculation due to the age of the child.

If none of the above applies to you, you should make an application for child maintenance to the Child Support Agency; the court cannot make an order for child maintenance in your case.

If you are not sure whether the court can hear your application please consult a solicitor; a member of the court staff may be able to assist you with the form, but cannot give you legal advice. Leaflet **D190 – I want to apply for a financial order** is also available.

What must I send to the court?

☐ Your completed divorce/dissolution/(judicial) separation petition – one for the court records and one service copy for the Respondent (and one service copy for the Co-Respondent, if applicable). You should keep a copy for your records.

☐ One original or certified marriage/civil partnership certificate – photocopies will not be accepted. (In cases of urgent applications it may be possible for you to provide an undertaking to the court to deliver the original or a certified copy of the marriage/civil partnership certificate to the court at a later date.)

☐ Your completed statement of arrangements for children, if applicable – one for the court records and one service copy for the Respondent. You should keep a copy for your records.

☐ The appropriate issue fee. Please see leaflet **EX50 – Civil and Family Court fees** for details on the fees payable and whether or not you have to pay them.